ORAL TRANSMISSION IN JUDAISM AND CHRISTIANITY

A Case for Memorization

THOMAS MEYER

CONTENTS

PREFACE

Utilizing an array of biblical, rabbinic, liturgical, historical and modern texts, I have attempted to outline the main features of oral transmission and memorization in the history of Judaism and Christianity. To understand the emphasis on memorization in Judaism and Christianity, I also investigated the surrounding cultures of Egypt, Assyria, Babylonia, and Greece to discern if their emphasis on memorization could have influenced the Jews and Christians.

During our investigation into memorization and Judaism in the Middle East, time will be spent exploring its importance in the biblical period (2000 BCE to 70 CE) and within that broad stroke, subdivisions include the First Temple Period (970-586 BCE) and the Second Temple Period (536-70 CE). The next period is the rabbinic period (1st to 6th century) with subdivisions into the Tannaitic (70 to 200 CE) and Amoraic periods (200-500 CE). The next period will be the medieval period (5th to 16th century) with a subdivision including the Geonic period (7th to 11th century), and finally the modern period (17th to 21st century).

During our investigation into memorization and Christianity in the Middle East, time will be spent exploring its importance in the early Church (1st to 3rd century), the Byzantine period (324-638), the medieval period (5th to 16th century), and the modern period (17th to 21st century).

The subject of this book is so vast, stretching over millennia, that we can offer only an encapsulation of the primary aspects of memorization in daily life. As the select bibliography indicates, each topic is a book in itself. Consequently, the research involved was more time consuming than writing. The research for this book took seven months. The project took much longer than anticipated, but upon finishing, I realized I had just begun. The footnotes and quotes attest to my dependence on the expertise of respected authors and living persons within Judaism and Christianity in Jerusalem. Aiming the book at both the specialist and non-specialist, I hope that in the process I have not missed either. In this book I turn not to strangers but to those followers of the Bible, whose hearts belong to it and who wish to know it more profoundly. I know that fewer people are won over by the written word than by the spoken word and that every great movement on this earth owes its growth more to great speakers than to great writers. Nevertheless, in order to produce more uniformity in the defense of this vital spiritual exercise, its fundamental principles must be committed to writing.

EVALUATION OF MODERN RESEARCH IN ORAL TRADITION

As we begin our journey let us first examine what place oral transmission and memorization of the Bible is given in the influential world of academia. Any scholarly research about memorizing the Bible and rabbinic literature is a consequence of study in the subject of oral tradition. There are many books on both oral and written transmission but none from my research that deal specifically with memorization. The absence of such books on memorization ought to tell us something of the value placed on it today in academia. I would like to highlight key individuals who have spearheaded the evaluation of modern research in oral tradition and by default memorization, and in doing so present a general consensus of what position academia holds today in regards to this subject.

The movement to pursue the study of religious oral tradition began in the 1950's. Ivan Engnell, professor of Old Testament studies in Uppsala from 1947-1963, aroused the ambition among students and colleagues to investigate the mysteries of oral and written transmission in Judaism and Christianity. Birger Gerhardsson, who attended Engell's seminar for several years, recognized the need to advance these inquiries further and was the first to study thoroughly the specific subject of oral and written transmission in rabbinic Judaism and early Christianity.

Gerhardsson's view of memorization and oral transmission in his 1961 book *Memory and Manuscript* repeats the views of modern day conservative Jewish and Christian scholars, that the ancients did indeed have the capability to memorize vast amounts of religious texts and did have the motive to hand them down orally without any major textual divergence until they were finally transmitted into writing. Gerhardsson constructed a model of the early sayings of Jesus in which memorization assumed the role of principal facilitator of the transmission process. Gerhardsson envisioned a mechanical commitment of oral and written texts to memory and a transmission by way of continual repetition which many of the primary rabbinic texts appropriate. He holds that the reason the sayings of Jesus had been kept faithfully until they were written was because of the memorization features Jesus used while he spoke; such as alliterations, proverbial diction, contrasts and antitheses, parallelism, rhythmic structures, and so on.

Gerhardsson interprets tractates regarding memorization from the Babylonian Talmud at face value, such as b. Gittin 60 as proof for valid testimonies concerning Second Temple period and earlier methods of Jewish memorization and oral transmission. He believed the literal meaning of what the ancients wrote regarding the necessity and their ability to memorize. The majority of modern scholarship does not hold such a view, that one can memorize the Scriptures in such large portions and would then choose to faithfully orally transmit those words, but believes that the structured speech associated with the Bible, rabbinic tradition, and early Christianity was later subject to the constructive and reconstructive work of social memory and thereby departed far from the original intent of the author.

Jacob Neusner, reshaped much of the scholarly discussion on our subject in the 1970's and 1980's by arguing that the maximalist positions were grounded in fundamental misconceptions about the nature of memorization in the transmission of oral tradition. Neusner's book *The Memorized Torah* from 1985 claims that oral tradition does not preserve the verbatim traditions, but rather the later stereotypical formulaic discourse of communities. He argued that the original forms of all the rabbinic writings are no longer retrievable. According to Neusner, maximalists had erred in two respects. First, they focused upon assumptions, rather than the redacted arrangement of literature into a complete unit, as the mnemonic foundation of oral tradition. Secondly, they employed a model of oral tradition that assumed an unchanging stability of oral material memorized verbatim and preserved without any major divergence throughout its history of oral transmission and transition to written form.

Neusner's model of rabbinic oral tradition recognizes its formulaic character as a mnemonic trick that preserves and transforms the tradition at the expense of its original wording. Accordingly, whatever might have been transmitted as oral tradition in rabbinic circles of the first and second centuries CE had been substantially erased by the mnemonically driven reformulations that were the price of their preservation. In short, Neusner's view is that the memorization of oral tradition behind rabbinic tradition was lost early in the process; what remained was the oral tradition preserved in and generated by the larger compositional units that had, from the second and third centuries CE, swallowed up the original forms of the tradition.[1]

In the 1990's Mary Carruthers's two books, *The Book of Memory* and *The Craft of Thought* were intent on enlarging conventional concepts of memory and the documentary culture of Christians in the medieval period. Examining medieval practices of reading, writing, meditation, and above all the function of memory and memory training she presented a religious and intellectual culture still rooted in practices that were fundamentally oral in nature though they lived in a printed world. She concluded that the culture of late antiquity and the medieval period must be viewed as a predominantly oral, rather than a purely written one.[2]

Most recently Martin Jaffee holds that rabbinic compilations are redacted anthologies whose compilers did not hesitate to alter the form and content of the previously handed down materials. In his book *Torah in the Mouth* from 2001 he holds that the scattered rabbinic texts were brought together, after complex transmissions, in diverse new orders depending upon the framework in which they were anthologized and the diverse degrees of redaction employed by their compilers. The compilation was a kind of freeze frame of that rabbinic tradition. But such activity was not conceived as the production of a finished "work." It was, at best, a "work in progress," finished only at the point that the views of its transmitters and users began to define the compilation as a text representing tradition itself rather than the ad- hoc storage place of tradition's texts.[3] According to Jaffee, the anthological model is a particularly apt compositional convention for a culture like that of classical rabbinic Judaism. He admits that rabbinic culture cultivated a strong oral-performance tradition, as attested by the countless instances in which disciples and rabbis are represented as engaging in discourse over a publicly recited text. At the same time, the orality of the rabbinic cultures intermeshed in numerous ways with scribal practices in which written texts were memorized and oral conventions of diction and formulation shaped what was written.[4] According to Jaffee, rabbinic oral tradition must be

---

1. Neusner, Jacob *The memorized Torah: The Mnemonic System of the Mishnah* pg. 58
2. Werner Kelber, *The Words of Memory* pg. 224
3. Martin Jaffee, *Oral Tradition in the Writings of the Rabbinic Oral Torah* pg. 22
4. ibid pg. 23

imagined as a diverse phenomenon, incorporating aspects of rote-memorization of documents and more fluid oral-performative aspects. The former activity, whether grounded in written transcripts or exclusively oral transmission remains unclear, was eventually used for mastery of the Mishnaic tractates alone. According to Jaffee, portions of the oral and written Torah would not be memorized verbatim, but could be retrieved for performance within the repertoire of mnemonically driven formulaic discourse that constituted the main oral-performative training of the student.[5]

Conclusion

What was discussed in Engell's seminar in the 1950's is today addressed again in academia. Issues concerning oral and written transmission and by default memorization have ever since been on the periphery of Biblical studies. New articles and books on oral transmission are being published and the subject is discussed at Christian and Jewish conferences and seminars. Yet, compared to the impressively productive memory work in the human and social sciences, memorization as a means of transmission and religious edification is by and large not perceived to be a pressing issue in current biblical scholarship. For example, the only instance in which memorization, conceived as a key concept, has entered the discourse world of New Testament scholarship was provided by Birger Gerhardsson's work *Memory and Manuscript* four decades ago. The conception of verbatim memorization and transmission of holy texts as key factors in oral transmission has been abandoned by the majority of scholars today. They hold that memorization and oral transmission are selective, and that the holy texts were greatly susceptible to change, flexibility, and degrees of improvisation.

Let me end this section with some food for thought, a story about oral transmission that can transfer us into the rest of the book. Mr. Hislop, the founder of a Christian missionary work in the East met his death by drowning in 1863. His official biography contains a detailed account of the incident, indicating how his horse arrived at a late hour at the motel at which he was awaited by his friends. A search discovered his body which had been carried some distance down a small stream which had been unexpectedly swollen by rains. When the time came to celebrate the 100 year anniversary of his arrival, some resolved to located more exactly the precise place at which he drowned. With the help of a map and the written record of his biography a small group went to retrace his last steps. It meant a cross country walk from the nearest road of about one mile. The explorers noted, however, to their perplexity that if the written transmission was accurate there seemed to have been no need for Mr. Hislop to have attempted to ford the stream in which he was said to have been drowned. A ride along its right bank was what was required of him.

When the explorers came near the spot which seemed to be indicated in the written record they called upon a local man working in the fields and asked him if he knew where it was that a European missionary had drowned three generations earlier. Without a moment's hesitation he set out to show them the exact place. As the group went along they were joined by several other villagers who also readily led them to the place in question. Very soon they indicated the place, a dry backwater fringed with trees and crossed by a track which indicated its regular use. This cleared up the difficulty left by the written transmission and fitted in with the oral testimony the villagers explained to them, namely, that it sometimes happened that the

---

5. ibid pg. 25

backwater filled up unexpectedly if there had been rain further up stream but none locally. The explorers had been given a blow for blow detailed oral account of the incident three generations later, so similar to what they had read that very morning when they prepared to make their search. Each detail tallied save one, and on that one point it was obvious that the oral transmission was correct and the written inaccurate. This incident left a remarkable impression on the explorers of the sheer accuracy of memorizing a story given the necessary conditions which were present in this case. The incident recalled made a deep impression on the people at that time. The death of a rare person would be an unusual sight and met this condition. Also the people concerned should be accustomed to rely on memory and what is heard and not to be dependent solely on written records.[6] This short account is an example of how given the right mixture of a slow paced, conservative community consisting of persons who live in an oral world, and hold to the importance of their text/story there is absolutely no reason to surmise that these persons do not have the ability and the motive to memorize verbatim and preserve their traditions in tact via oral transmission for their own edification and future oral transmission.

6. *The Expository Times 1957* pg. 284

CHAPTER I

When the World was Oral:
History of Oral Tradition and Memorization

In this chapter we want to start with a background of when the world was oral and dominated by memorization and orality before we narrow our emphasis on Judaism and Christianity. We want first to step back and trace the importance of the oral story, the spoken word, and the exercise of memorization in cultures within the sphere of influence of Judaism to determine as well as speculate how these cultures' emphasis on orality may have affected Judaism's emphasis on memorization.

General Description

Long before any story had been transmitted to writing, there existed only oral literature delivered from memory and transmitted orally from person to person. Without the story we do not have human identity. There are stories surviving from every human era and almost every social group known to us, if not frozen in writing then frozen in burial tomb portrayals. This is because we identify humanity in others by hearing their stories. Today a text read well, but especially recited from memory regains some of its original oral authority and impact. God did not write to Moses but spoke to him. The sense of the spoken word as divine power is especially vivid in the foundational accounts of diverse peoples, ancient and modern, in all parts of the world. Accounts of the origin of the world ascribe the initial creative act to the spoken divine word, not only in the opening of Genesis and John but also the creative word of Ptah in ancient Egyptian mythology.[1]

The traditions of an oral society had the advantage of an undeniable intimacy and directness with the divine word which are somewhat lost when the stories are written down. Putting words down permanently in writing places them outside the heart, while the seat of emotion lies inside the heart. A literate culture can indeed have a rich and imaginative religious literature, but its dependence on the written word alone inevitably creates distance between the community and its faith and practice.[2] The greater part of ancient literature was intended for the ears more than the eyes. Yet, the replacement of oral transmission by use of the written word has been the repeated uniform pattern of historical development across all geographical and cultural boundaries, even though the variation of how long or late this occurs is quite large.[3]

To understand this very special aspect of oral transmission and memorization we must momentarily forget our technological civilization and its way of life. For us setting thought down in a permanent and material form so that it can be found again in an unaltered state are acts that seem so natural to us that we can scarcely imagine societies that were able to do without them almost entirely. Thought was handed down

---

1. William Graham, *Beyond the Written Word* pg. 64
2. Antoinette Clark *Wire, Holy Lives, Holy Deaths. A Closer Hearing of Early Jewish Storytellers* pg. 1
3. William Graham, *Beyond the Written Word* pg. 59

in the most lasting and permanent manner, in the same way God created the world, by the spoken word.[4]

The emphasis on memorization was an anthropological phenomenon among cultures that influenced Jewish thought and practice. The mind or heart stood at the center of the oral-written crossing point in the regions within their sphere of influences. The focus on these surrounding cultures was on inscribing their most precious traditions on the insides of their people. Within this context, copies of texts served as solidified reference points for recitation and memorization of their respective traditions.[5]

Like today, such tasks of vast memorization were not for the unskilled. Like today few of the literates would have progressed to the point where they would have been able or motivated enough to memorize such vast texts verbatim. There are many parallels in the cultures of Egypt, Assyria, Babylonia and Greece in regards to the fundamental emphasis on memorization. Small scale kingdoms like Israel and Judah maintained educational and scribal systems that often emulated their neighbors and borrowed their mnemonic techniques while working in a larger sphere of oral tradition. Let us examine the above mentioned cultures and see if their emphasis on memorization could have influenced or have been borrowed by the Jewish people.

Memorization in Ancient Egypt

In the intermixed oral-written environment of the New Kingdom in Ancient Egypt, our textual evidence regarding their educational process is meager. We have some ostraca and reused papyri, almost exclusively from the 16th to 11th century New Kingdom found at Deir el-Medina. We lack widespread examples of upper-level educational texts, many of which were written on perishable wooden boards and papyri. The earliest and most prominent forms of education appear to have involved the temple and family based learning like we later observe in Ancient Israel.[6] We do know that Egyptian education stressed copying, memorization, and recitation of their core curriculum. The goal of memorization is reflected in various ways in the Egyptian texts. The *Instruction of Ptahhotep* concludes with an injunction to listen to the written word, including a promise that this memory will preserve the oral tradition: *"Memory of (the teaching's maxims) will not depart from the mouths of man, because of the perfection of their verses."*[7]

One key mnemonic used in the Egyptian memorization process was training students to sing or chant texts like we observe later in Judaism during the time of Isaiah (chapter 28). Most of the core texts appear to have been composed for oral performance, with the use of metrical and repetitive structures to facilitate the memory. Many exercises include the first line of the following section so that students memorizing individual texts can put them in the correct order. A New Kingdom polemic against existing modes of education describes the process: *"You have come here loaded with great secrets. You have cited a verse from Hardjedef. You do not know, however, whether it is intended as good or bad, which stanza is before it, which after it. You are a skilled scribe at the head of his fellows, and the teaching of every book is written on your heart."*[8] In another text, Amenemope depicts his writings as oral when calling on his son to "hear" his

4. William Schniedewind, *How the Bible became a book* pg. 16
5. David Carr, *Writing on the Tablet of the Heart* pg. 6
6. ibid pg. 65
7. ibid pg. 72
8. ibid pg. 73

instruction, and he uses metaphors for memorization such as *"let them rest in the casket of your belly, may they be bolted in your heart"*[9] which are later prevalent in the Proverbs of Solomon.

Like in later Judaism, the goal of the Egyptian scribal student was memorized mastery of the cultural tradition. In the New Kingdom text, *Instruction of Any*, Any calls on his son to memorize written wisdom, to *"study the writings, put them on your heart."* Yet the writing concludes with a debate between him and his son, in which his son points out that learning based on writings is incomplete for those who do not understand them, for *"a son thinks poorly in himself when he merely recites sayings from books."*[10] He goes on to make a contrast between truly internalized teachings and those that are merely mouthed by memory: *"When your words are pleasing in the heart, the heart inclines to receive them. Then the heart rejoices in the abundance of your virtues, and thoughts are lifted up to you. A boy cannot perform the moral teachings when the books are merely on his tongue."*[11] The notion of memorizing a text solely as religiously edifying but not knowing its contents is a phenomenon we will later see practiced in rabbinic Judaism. Egyptian sacred texts were memorized with a copy deposited in a "house of life" for safekeeping like we see later in the Jewish Temple. There was also an emphasis on "hearing" and inscribing teachings on the heart with a focus on orality and memorization.

What little we do know about education during the New Kingdom places a tremendous emphasis on memorization and the orality of texts. It is tempting to infer what influence the New Kingdom of Egypt's education system and emphasis on memorization had on the Israelites who lived there for 430 years. Did the Jews borrow the model of home-school education from the Egyptians? Did the emphasis on memorization Moses received in Egyptian schools prepare him to be able to gather, memorize and retain all the sources he needed to compose the Torah from memory? Did Moses pass these mnemonic techniques of oral transmission down to certain individuals among the children of Israel?

Memorization in Ancient Assyria and Babylon

Like Egypt, the students of Assyria and Babylon often learned through a process of dictation, memorization, and recitation. The teacher tells the student in one dialogue, *"repeat it to me, say everything to me exactly."*[12] Another dialogue has a student say, *"I explained my exercise tablets to my father, recited my table to him, and he was delighted."*[13] Ultimately, the goal was for the successful Assyrian or Babylonian student to become a scribe and be able to both write down and accurately recite the lists and standard stories that were the foundation of their education and culture. This included memorization of extensive sign lists, name lists, treaties, hymns and epics, and so on. A student in one dialogue boasts he *"can give the 600 signs in their correct order"* and *"my teacher had to show me a sign only once, and I could add several from memory."*[14] The emphasis on memorization was not just for students, the Assyrian King Ashurbanipal in the 7th century asks a blessing from Shamash on anyone who memorizes his hymn and performs it. We read in

---

9. ibid pg. 74
10. ibid pg. 75
11. ibid pg. 75
12. ibid pg. 27
13. ibid pg. 75
14. ibid pg. 23

the benediction: *"Whosoever shall learn this text by heart and glorify the judge of the Gods, Shamash, may he make his enemies precarious, may the word of his mouth please the people."[15]*

From tablet 7 of Enuma Elish which describes the fifty names of the Babylonian god Marduk we read: *"The sage and the learned shall together ponder them, father shall tell of them to son and recite them to him."[16]* The total may well have run into tens of thousands of lines for some students to memorize. These ancient cultures were enthusiastic about writing; but we have texts that still stress the importance attached to learning by heart. From the Irra myth we find: *"The scribe who learns this text by heart escapes the enemy, is honored in his own land. In the congregation of the learned where my name is constantly spoken I will open his ears."[17]* These ancient scribes had memorized their traditions and could use those earlier memorized texts as mental prototypes, reusing them, recombining them, and later adapting them in the process of creating new texts. Though they were capable of reading and copying an ancient tablet, they did not necessarily need to. The primary mode of existence of such ancient texts was not written tablets but the tablet of the heart of well trained scribes.[18] Like Egypt it is tempting to infer what influence the Assyrian and Babylonian education system and emphasis on memorization had on those who were deported in 721, those who later lived amidst the Assyrian presence in the north, and those who were carried away into exile from 605-586: *"teach them the learning of the Babylonians"* (Daniel 1:4).

Memorization in Ancient Greece

Memorization and her virtues were well acknowledged by Greek mythology. Mnemosyne, the goddess of memory, had born Zeus nine daughters, the Muses, who personified and presided over different modes of the arts and sciences. This myth of Mnemosyne and her Muses articulates the centrality of memory in Greek culture. As mother of the Muses, Mnemosyne was the origin of all artistic and scientific labors and the wellspring of civilization. From the perspective of that myth, it was not writing, nor logic or rhetoric that was perceived to be the central agency, but memorization.[19] We have little epigraphic evidence from ancient Greece that helps us to know what kind of techniques the Greeks used to memorize and what stress was laid on memorization. Much of what we know about 3rd and 4th century B.C.E. Greek education comes from the writings of Plato. In *Protagoras and Laws*, Plato has Protagoras describe early education as follows: *"When boys have learned their letters and are ready to understand the written word as formerly the spoken, they set the works of great poets next to them to read and make them learn them by heart."[20]* Among the Greek student's goals was to have texts written on the tablet of their heart. Toward this end, teachers and authors provided memory helps for students. For example, in Aristotle's work *On Memory* we see the recommendation that students link items in a series to letters in the alphabet, using the alphabet sequence learned early in education as a structure on which to hang more complex memorized texts gained later on.[21] In Homer there are numerous elements that would have aided memorization: use of standard sequences,

---

15. Eduard Nielsen, *Oral Tradition* pg. 20
16. ibid pg. 20
17. Eduard Nielsen, *Oral Tradition* pg. 19
18. David Carr, *Writing on the Tablet of the Heart* pg. 40
19. Werner Kelber, *The Words of Memory* pg. 222
20. David Carr, *Writing on the Tablet of the Heart* pg. 49
21. Mary Carruthers, *Book of Memory* pg. 109

repetition of the same sequence, repetition of broader speeches, and so on.

It is well known the influence that Hellenism had on Jewish culture. It is written from the 1st century in rabbinic sources that: *"Permission was given to the House of Rabban Gamaliel to teach their children Greek owing to their relation to the Roman government"* (b. Sota 49b). Again from the 1st century: *"there were a 1000 young men in my father's house, 500 of who studied the Torah, while the other 500 studied Greek wisdom"* (b. Sota 49b). In the Talmud it records that in the Hellenized town of Caesarea there were Jews who read the Shema in Greek (b. Sota 21b). The rabbis spoke to the people in Aramaic, but in the midst of their homilies they often inserted Greek words (j. Keth. 31d). The Greek language and educational methods took hold of all classes among all nations on the Mediterranean Sea board. The Jewish world was no exception in this respect. Almost everything Greek penetrated deep into all the classes of Jewish society.[22] The emphasis placed on memorization and its mnemonic techniques in Greek education would have undoubtedly been incorporated into the already existing orally dominated Jewish education system. To what extent Greek memorization techniques were adopted by the Jewish people and if there was a revival of memorization due to Greek influence we do not know.

Conclusion

The civilizations which influenced many of the writers and cultures of the Bible were assertive about the necessity of memorization as we have clearly seen from their own primary sources. In the above mentioned cultures, memorization and the student's heart were the key focus in teaching texts as we see later in Judaism. Memorizable texts carried many epithets, formulized stanzas, expressions and clichés which were valued as memory aids and characteristics that fit ancient oral cultures. Oral communication has always had a tendency to be very conservative and traditionalist. While writing freezes information so that it can be preserved without great effort, orality must rely on memory and repetition to preserve valuable information and therefore gives more weight to traditional wisdom than to new ideas. Just as the Egyptian *Satiric Letter* spoke of the addressee as *"having the teaching of every book inscribed on his heart"* and several Greek texts spoke of having texts *"written on the tablet of the heart,"* so also Jewish literature joined textuality and memorization in this way.

---

22. Saul Liberman, *Greek in Jewish Palestine* pg. 39

CHAPTER II

An Overview of Jewish Oral Tradition and Memorization in the Middle East

We have already seen how important memorization was in the oral world that influenced Jewish thought and practice before the time of Christianity and the numerous possibilities of how those cultures directly or indirectly influenced Judaism's emphasis on orality and memorization. In this chapter we want to trace systematically the importance of memorization and oral transmission in the Hebrew world from the time of Ancient Israel through the Second Temple period, the rabbinic period, the medieval period and the modern period in the Middle East.

Memorization and Orality in Ancient Israel

Spoken words in Ancient Israel as well as neighboring regions were not merely means of communication but objects of power. Words spoken by God, priests, prophets, and poets were believed to possess divine power. Once uttered, such words could take on everlasting life. For example, God spoke the curse to the serpent and Noah spoke the cursing of Canaan. Isaac recognized that he had been deceived into blessing Jacob but his culture did not allow him to revoke the oral blessing.

The Patriarchs apparently lived in an oral world and thereby relied heavily upon memorized oral contracts. Cases brought before tribal sheiks like Abraham and Jacob were argued orally and decided on the basis of well known customs. Oral testimony was taken, and judgments were announced and held in the memory of those who heard. For example, Abraham's purchase of the cave of Machpelah is described as a purely oral arrangement in the company of witnesses. When Jacob seeks to be reunited with Esau he first sends a spoken message. In this orally dominant society, the ability to speak effectively was a prerequisite for leadership. A chief did not have to be able necessarily read or write, but did have to be able to make himself clearly heard and understood. Therefore, Moses tried to reject God's order by arguing that he had uncircumcised lips and would be an ineffective communicator to Pharaoh.

Among the early Israelite tribes there was likely a family of specialists, speakers, and trained memorizers who had mastered and practiced the art of the recitation of their stories and was prepared to speak these accounts at appropriate ceremonies; as Moses did on the other side of the Jordan, and Joshua at Shechem. Through these songs, stories, and proverbial sayings the oral traditions were memorized and passed along to the next generation. Even the Ten Commandments were given orally to Israel, the account actually never mentions writing the Commandments down: *"And God spoke all these words"* (Exodus 20:1). The omission of writing reflects an oral word and time of memorization and oral transmission.[23]

---

23. Daniel Jeremy Silver, *The Story of Scripture* pg. 47

The books of Deuteronomy and Joshua provide us with numerous references to the Torah being spoken aloud to the community through recitation and public readings. It was through these oral exercises that memorization was made possible to the people of ancient Israel.[24] We will later see a parallel example of this phenomenon when Josephus claims that those who heard the public reading of Scripture in the 1st century CE were able to memorize and retain what they heard through public readings. Deuteronomy chapters 31-32 record the eventual writing down of the Torah. The teachings uttered orally and memorized were now being fixed in writing by Moses himself as he neared death. The necessity to write down oral tradition because of a crisis is a theme that threads itself through Judaic and Christian traditions.

The main moral concern once Joshua entered the land was with the spiritual condition of the people's heart. A well stocked and active mind, full of memorized Torah, was held to be the mother of virtue, because what was in a person's heart inevitably showed up in their actions. Therefore God commanded Joshua and all Israel: *"This book of the Torah shall not depart out of your mouth but you shall meditate on it day and night, that thou may observe to do according to all that is written therein, then shall you make your way prosperous then shall you have good success"* (Joshua 1:8).

Memorization of the Torah and virtue were inextricably linked in the Jewish mind. The ancient Israelites associated intelligence with memorization, retention and obedience to Torah. The Bible is full of admonitions to recite God's instructions lest they be forgotten: *"Recite these instructions when you stay at home and when you are away, when you lie down and when you get up"* (Dt. 6.7). In the time of the Judges we find no explicit mention in the Bible urging Israel to memorize the Torah like we hear in Joshua, though we still have statements of oral contracts in the book of Ruth that indicate they still lived in an oral world. It is not until the 10th century in the time of David and Solomon that we have multiple commands to *"hide God's Word in your heart so you do not sin against him"* (Psalm 119:11), and to *"bind the Torah around your fingers, write it upon the table of our heart"* (Proverbs 3). After the 10th century writings there are very few clear commands or inferences to memorize the Scriptures throughout the rest of the Tenach. It is not until we get to the Second Temple period that we see a reemergence of memorization in Jewish literature.

Memorization in the Babylonian Exile

The Jewish Temple and many major religious and administrative centers were destroyed by the Babylonians from 605-586 as well as the deportation of many classes of society. It is unclear how the Jews in Babylon would have had access to the written versions of their Scriptures in captivity. Memorization must have played a key role in keeping hope and the traditions alive in exile. Scribes likely had little or no access to authoritative copies of the Scriptures and may not have had any alternative but to produce "new" written copies strictly from memory for liturgical and private use.

Memorization in the Second Temple Period

The emphasis on memorization in Jewish society reemerged strong in the Second Temple Period. Whether or not the 3rd century B.C.E. story of how the Septuagint came into being is factual or not does not concern us here. It is written in the Talmud: *"It has been taught: It once happened that King Ptolemy*

---

24. Joachim Schaper, *The Living Word Engraved in Stone* pg. 16

gathered 72 elders and put them into 72 chambers without telling them why he had assembled them. He went to each one and said: Write out for me the Torah of your teacher Moses. God put counsel into the heart of every one of them, and they all agreed upon the same text and wrote (from memory the whole Torah)…" (b. Megilla 9a). The point that interests us is that in the oral world of 3rd century Alexandria it was plausible for scribes to write out the whole Torah from memory. The author of the 2nd century B.C.E. text 2 Maccabees presents his own Greek text as a possible focal point for memorization, with the author crafting the text *"to please those who wish to read, to make it easy for those who are inclined to memorize"* (2 Macc. 2:25). How the author structured the text of 2 Maccabees to make it easy for those who are inclined to memorize we do not know, we just know he did. The author of the 2nd century B.C.E. book of Jubilees presents the ability of memorization as a gift from God: *"And Jacob said: Lord, how can I remember all that I have read and seen? And he said unto him: I will bring all things to thy remembrance. And he went up from him, and he awoke from his sleep, and he remembered everything which he had read and seen, and he wrote down all the words (from memory) which he had read and seen"* (Jubilees 32:24-26). The Wisdom of Ben Sira from the 2nd century B.C.E. shows an unbroken chain of resemblance to the data seen in earlier Israel in regards to memorization. Ben Sira like Solomon, urges students to lay his teachings to their heart in order to become wise (50:27-29). It is interesting that in the 2nd century BCE the heart is still considered the medium on which wisdom was to be inscribed. Such memorization of Ben Sira's written instruction was facilitated by its use of internal mnemonics (25:1-2). Later, Ben Sira's grandson describes him as one who not only read *"the law, prophets, and other writings of our ancestors"* but also memorized them, having *"gained possession for himself"* of these writings.[25]

Though memorization was widespread, by the time of the 1st century B.C.E. the strictest rules governed the handling, the reading and the copying of the written Torah. Multiplication of copies by oral dictation was not technically allowed. Each scroll had to be copied directly from another scroll. Official copies, until 70 C.E. derived from a master copy in the Temple. As always, there existed an attitude of concern for preserving the precise wording of the inspired text. The rule that the sacred books must be read in the synagogue and not recited by memory contributed to the safeguarding of the exact wording of the text, though the *targumim* recited the translated text from memory to the audience.[26] More will be written about the role of the *hazzan* and *targumim* in a later section.

Josephus's descriptions often focus on education in the Torah, which he asserts is the foundation of 1st century Jewish education. As a result of their religious education, Josephus claims Jews can recite the Torah from memory *"more easily than their own name."*[27] Their thorough grounding in Torah from early on had ensured that the laws were engraved on their hearts. Josephus describes the seventh-year reading of the Torah to all the people at the Feast of Tabernacles as resulting in its being *"graven on their hearts and stored in the memory so that they can never be effaced"* or *"so graven on their hearts through the hearing of that which they command that they will forever carry within them the principles of the regulations."*[28]

---

25. David Carr, *Writing on the Tablet of the Heart* pg. 209
26. P.R. Ackroyd, *The Cambridge History of the Bible vol. 1* pg. 50
27. Josephus, *Ant. 4:211*
28. ibid *Ant. 4:210*

We read here a continuation of the practice of the larger populace memorizing the Torah via oral proclamations in social settings.

Everyone is familiar with the different sects of Judaism in the first century, but did they emphasize memorization? Let us start with the Pharisees. Just who the Pharisees were is not an easy question to answer. They have left no writings of their own, so there is no firsthand evidence from which to imagine the details of their religious world. We are entirely dependent upon what the New Testament and ancient writers such as Josephus chose to record about them.[29] The New Testament often mentions the Pharisees as keeping "the traditions of men" which were rabbinic oral traditions that were the foundation for the later composition of the Mishnah. Josephus also mentions the Pharisaic oral tradition: *I wish merely to explain that the Pharisees had passed on to the people certain regulations handed down by former generations and not recorded in the Law of Moses, for which reason they are rejected by the Sadducean group, who held that only those regulations should be considered valid which were written down, and that those which had been handed down by former generations need not to be observed."[30]*

The Saducean group has left us no writings, and the positions concerning whether or not the Essenes were those who lived at the Qumran community or not are well known and will not be addressed here. But in regards to the Qumran community, several aspects confirm that written Torah traditions were used as part of an oral-written process for memorization-education. Many Torah and non-Torah texts were clearly copied in the Qumran community. Thus many features of the finds at Qumran, such as manuscript errors and Torah quotes, reading divisions in Torah manuscripts, and production of new formulations of Torah traditions through use of prior memorized versions, reflect the phenomenon of memorization. An oral-written instructional text found at Qumran used in education stresses memorization: *"You have preserved your Torah before me, and your covenant has been confirmed for me, and you have prevailed over my heart to walk in your paths. You have called my heart to attention and my kidneys you sharpened, so that they did forget your laws"* (4Q Barki Napshi). This passage plays on the word used in Deuteronomy 6:7 for constant recitation of Torah, in describing how God has sharpened the speaker's kidneys so that he does not forget the words of the Torah.[31] We are nowhere told what mnemonic techniques any of the Jewish sects utilized to memorize and preserve the Bible and their oral traditions in the first century.

Let us continue tracing the first century and observe the beginnings of the rabbinic movement. After the destruction of the Temple in 70 CE, the first claim that someone had received a tradition in the precise language in which it was formulated, memorized and orally transmitted comes from Yohanan b. Zakkai: *"R. Joshua said, I have heard as a tradition from Rabban b. Zakai, who heard from his teacher, and his teacher from his teacher, as a halacha given to Moses from Sinai, that Elijah will not come to declare unclean or clean"* (M. Eduyyot 8:3). Around the time of the founding of the rabbinic center at Yavneh comes the first claim that someone has accurate oral traditions of the essential content of the oral Torah. Following the generation of Yavneh in the 2nd century come claims that these traditions were not merely of the content, but the exact words memorized and handed from Mt. Sinai. Yavneh was the place of the origin both of clearly defined rabbinic literary forms and mnemonically structured memorizable rabbinic teachings. It was

29. Martin Jaffee, *Early Judaism* pg. 79
30. Josephus, *Ant. 13:277*
31. David Carr, *Writing on the Tablet of the Heart* pg. 237

probably R. Akiva in the early 1st century who fully developed this movement, for it was he who set forth the foundations of the Mishnah, and it was in his time that the institution of the *tanna*, or official memorizer, is first mentioned.[32] What evidence we have of memorization and oral transmission from 2 Maccabees, Jubilees, Ben Sira, and Josephus leads us to believe that memorization was still the linchpin in Jewish thought and practice during the Second Temple Period and as we shall see took off to new heights during the rabbinic period.

Memorization in the Rabbinic Period

The Mishnah which is translated as "repeated tradition," was the first and foremost oral text in the early rabbinic period. It is an ancient book of case law that was codified in 200 C.E. but existed well before 70 CE. The Mishnah provides a set of norms that defines Jewish communal life in the ritual, civil, and criminal domains which all religious Jews had to memorize and be intimately acquainted with in order to keep kosher. Its appearance marked a new achievement in the history of systematizing oral Jewish law, creating a model for the other important codes of Jewish law that would follow. In the years before and following its compilation the Mishnah became the central text in the rabbinic curriculum of sacred study and memorization. Around the time of the Mishnah's appearance, the ever growing corpus of rabbinic teachings came to be known as oral Torah. The term Torah indicated that this body of teachings was taken to be divine instruction, and the specification "oral" distinguished it from the written Torah. Whereas the written Torah was already fixed in writing, the oral Torah was memorized and unfolded in an ongoing oral manner through debate, dialogue, and argumentation.

The discussions centered on the Mishnah eventually produced another oral manifestation called the Talmud. The two Talmuds (Palestinian, c. 370-425 C.E., and Babylonian, c. 600 C.E.), which record the accumulated oral wisdom of the rabbinic movement were organized as commentaries around the skeletal structure of the Mishnah.[33]

Let us examine a principal text concerning oral transmission and memorization of the oral Torah in the Babylonian Talmud (b. Eruvin 54b): *"Our Masters repeated this tradition: How is the Repeated Tradition arranged for transmission? Moses learned it from the mouth of the Omnipotent. Aaron entered and Moses repeated for him his chapter. Aaron retired and sat toward the left of Moses. Aaron's sons Eleazar and Itamar entered and Moses repeated for them their chapter. His sons retired, Eleazar sitting to the right of Moses and Itamar to the left of Aaron. Rabbi Yehudah says: Aaron always remained at the right of Moses. The (70) Elders entered and Moses repeated for them their chapter. The Elders retired. All the nation entered and Moses repeated for them their chapter. The result is that Aaron acquired four repetitions, his sons acquired three, the Elders acquired two, and all the nation acquired one. Then Moses retired and Aaron repeated for them his chapter. Then Aaron retired and his sons repeated for them their chapter. Then his sons retired and the Elders repeated for them their chapter. The result is that all acquired four repetitions. On this basis said Rabbi Eliezer: A person is obliged to repeat traditions to his disciples four times. And this follows logically: Just as Aaron learned from the mouth of Moses, and Moses learned from the mouth of the*

32. Jacob Neusner, *The Rabbinic Tradition about the Pharisees before 70* pg. 14
33. Jacob Neusner, *Oral Tradition in Judaism* pg. 17

Omnipotent, doesn't it follow that mere mortals who learn from mere mortals should do so as well? Rabbi Akiva says: Where do we learn that a person is obliged to repeat for his disciples indefinitely until they learn (memorize)? For it is said: And teach it to the children of Israel (Dt. 31.19). And where do we learn to teach it until it is fluent in their mouths as memorized texts? For it is said: And place it in their mouths (Dt. 31.19). And where do we learn that he is obliged to show him other perspectives on the memorized text? For it is said: Now these are the rulings that you should present before them (Ex. 21.1)."

According to rabbinic theology, Moses received the Torah from God at Mount Sinai and the divine revelation came to him for transmission in two media. One was the Torah in writing and the other was the oral Torah, which was received and then transmitted via the medium of memorization until it reached a written published form ages later. The Hebrew phrase translated as "oral Torah" means "that which is memorized" hence one may speak of "the memorized Torah." The above mentioned Talmudic text wants the listener to know how the repeated oral tradition was taught for many reasons; so one may trust its reliability and so that the listener may mimic it. We learn from this text that the oral Torah was taught by the student's listening to the words of a teacher and repeating his memorized words verbatim. The pedagogical model established at this time was the basis for rabbinic instruction. The oral tradition surviving among the rabbis was transmitted in the original way, by patient repetition, from master to disciple, from mouth to ear, and from ear to memory without being written.[34]

As a matter of principle, the Mishnah and Talmud were themselves to be transmitted solely in the context of a memorized performance. Such written copies as may have existed technically were banned from use. This censure was based on a prohibition issued at the latest in 3rd century Palestine, which forbade anyone to commit the oral tradition to writing or to use a text in memorizing. The prohibition on writing oral Torah must have existed for some time. Thus it is likely that during the 3rd century the prohibition on writing the oral Torah was being put to the test, and thus necessitated its explicit reinforcement. We read in the Tosefta (a *halakhic* collection similar to, but larger than, the Mishnah, edited anonymously by 300 CE in Palestine): *"Written benedictions, even if they have letters from the name of God and include many topics from the Torah, are not to be saved from a fire which broke out on the Sabbath, but are left to burn in their place. Thus the Masters said: Those who write benedictions are like those who burn the Torah. There was a case of one who wrote down benedictions, and this was reported to R. Yishmael who went to examine him. When R. Yishmael was coming up the ladder, he felt his presence, took the collection of benedictions and put them in a bowl of water. Thereupon R. Yishmael spoke to him in this language: The punishment for the last deed is more severe than for the first"* (t. Shabb. 13.4). It was forbidden even to write benedictions during the rabbinic period, everything was to be transmitted orally. We also read in the Tosefta: *"It once happened that R. Halafta went to R. Gamliel in Tiberias and found him sitting at the table of Yohanan ben Nazif. In his hand was a targum of the book of Job, which he was reading. Said R. Halafta to him: I remember Rabban Gamliel the Elder, your father's father, sitting on the stairs of the Temple, when they brought a targum of the book of Job before him. He spoke to the boulder, and they hid it under a row of stones"* (t. Sofrim 14:2).

We have seen in the early rabbinic period an emphasis on memorization of texts by oral transmission from teacher to student. The opposition during this orally dominant period was to the use of any written

---

34. Martin S. Jaffee, *Torah in the Mouth* pg. 4

halacha texts. We continue to see the thread of memorization which started in Ancient Israel as the dominant thread holding together Jewish thought and practice.

Some 200 years after the Mishnah was codified, the work of Abba Arika marked the culmination of the oral transmission on the Babylonian Talmud. The time had now come when the preservation and arrangement of the oral materials already collected were more important than any further additions. Nahman b. Isaac in the 4th century, pupil and successor of Raba described the task of the compilers of the Talmud in the following words: *"I am neither a sage nor a seer, nor even a scholar as contrasted with the majority. I am a transmitter (gamrana) and an arranger (sadrana)"* (b. Pes. 105b). It is clear that Nahman b. Isaac actually engaged in the task of oral redaction from the fact that he is mentioned as the sage who introduced the memorization technique of mnemonics to the Jewish people, which was designed to facilitate the memorizing and grouping of the sea of Talmudic passages. The material was now ready for its final redaction and was orally edited at the Academy of Sura in Babylon.[35] When exactly the Talmud was transmitted into writing we do not know but it nevertheless continued to be regarded as an oral text to be memorized and orally proclaimed.

Memorization in the Geonic Period

The Talmud continued to be memorized and studied orally even after it was published in the post-Talmudic period, from the 7th to 11th centuries. Though written transmission was starting to triumph over orality in many rabbinic colleges in Babylonia there was still a great emphasis on memorization. R. Natronai Gaon in the 9th century reported that after morning prayers, the yeshiva divided into two groups, those whose primary concern was Talmud, and those who were primarily memorizers, who then occupied themselves with Mishnah, Midrash and Tosefta. These were living books, the *Garsae* (learners or memorizers) whose function it was to recite the Talmud by heart to the students and scholars in the Babylonian Colleges.[36] R. Aaron Sargado in the 10th century noted that *"our yeshiva, of which it is known that its version of the Talmud is from the mouths of the great ones...most of the members of the yeshiva do not know anything of a book"* (b. Yev. 39b). Why did the Geonim maintain this difficult system of memorization of large bodies of text in an era when orality was giving way to textuality? R. Aaron argues for the superiority of the school's version of the Talmudic text on the basis of its unbroken oral tradition which reaches back to the 3rd century. Oral transmission was not only the proper way of doing things to them, it was considered more reliable than written transmission.[37]

From the 10th century on there is an almost complete dearth of direct witness for the ancient rabbinic works. We have no knowledge of the oral transmission and memorization of ancient texts during this period from direct sources.[38] Be that as it may, opinions differ regarding how and when the various compilations of oral teaching came to be written down. The writings in manuscript form stemmed faithfully from memorized teachings that for centuries had been inscribed only in the memories of rabbis and transmitted solely in the oral instruction imparted by rabbis to their students after the fashion of the instruction give in Eruvin 54b.

35. *Jewish Encyclopedia vol. 13* pg. 19
36. Daphna Ephrat, *Orality and the Institutionalization of Tradition: Transmitting Jewish Tradition* pg. 111
37. ibid pg. 114
38. Paul Mandel, *Between Byzantium and Islam: Transmitting Jewish Tradition* pg. 75

Memorization in the Medieval Period

Existence in written form did not for the medievalist preclude a text from falling into the category of oral Torah. What made a text oral was neither the medium of its form nor the fact that mastery of the text involved the capacity to call its sources immediately to mind.[39] Medieval rabbinic intellectuals viewed the written copy as an almost accidental present, a material object which belonged in the memory of the student not in a book on the shelf. It was theory, not reading practice that distinguished oral from written in the medieval rabbinic mind. Medieval rabbinic scholars believed that their commitment to memorization replicated the handing down of the original Sinaitic revelation we previously read about (b. Eruvin 54b). In their thinking, a crucial portion of the revelation had remained unwritten and necessarily committed to memory. To memorize now was to take one's place within a chain of oral learning millennia old.

The sources available to medieval scholars placed great emphasis on continuing the unwritten, exclusively oral nature of the tradition in the present. Jewish mystics in the medieval period referred to their teaching as *qabbalah,* derived etymologically from the word *qibbel* (to receive) which connotes reception of a practice that has been transmitted orally. They claimed their kabbalistic traditions were passed down by word of mouth starting from Elijah in the 8th century B.C.E. Memorization played a vital role in the transmission of kabbalistic texts and was required as a prerequisite for understanding its doctrine. According to a 13th century text: *"R. Sherira and R. Hai, blessed be their memory, were competent in and received this science as a tradition transmitted in their hands, master from the mouth of master, and sage from the mouth of sage, a gaon from the mouth of a gaon."*[40] Another 13th century text traces the chain of oral transmission of the knowledge of God's name from Abraham to the medieval period: *"From that time until now there has not been in Israel any generation that has not received the tradition of wisdom (from memory), which is knowledge of the name, through the order of the tradition, the oral Torah."*[41] The writing down of doctrine would prove to be dangerous for kabbalists insofar as it would lead to the misunderstanding of their sensitive theological issues. Nevertheless the threat of forgetfulness was so strong that putting the doctrines into writing was inevitable: *"Verily, at this time that which was hidden has been revealed because forgetfulness has reached its limit, and the end of forgetfulness is the beginning of remembrance."*[42] Once again we see that it was necessary at a certain point to transmit into writing the oral tradition for fear it would be lost. Also though there was an option to go full fledged into written transmission, the Jewish people continued to memorize and pass down orally their traditions. They considered the oral to be more reliable than the written transmission.

Memorization in the Modern Period

In order to get an idea of what emphasis is put on memorization of the oral and written Torah in the world of Judaism in the modern period I interviewed different rabbis, students, and a professional cantor. I am going to wait until a later section to explain their testimonies on the orality of Judaism today and the emphasis put on memorization from the classroom to the synagogue.

39. Martin Jaffee, *Oral Tradition in the Writing of Rabbinic Oral Torah* pg. 8
40. Moshe Idel, *Transmission in Thriteeenth-Century Kabbalah: Transmitting Jewish Tradition* pg. 143
41. Elliot Wolfson, *Transmission in Medieval Mysticism: Transmitting Jewish Tradition* pg. 178
42. ibid pg. 184

14

Conclusion

As we have clearly seen the Jewish people have always held memorization and orality in high regard during all periods. Even before there was a written torah or an oral version of it for that matter the Patriarchs moved and lived in an oral world. We saw the emphasis put on memorizing and hiding God's Word in your heart in the 10th century BCE and the same influence alive and well in the Second Temple Period. We saw how integral orality and memorization were to daily life in the rabbinic period. Their whole world was oral. The Jewish people have historically opted to stay in an oral world when the world around them was moving towards the written. We read that the reason for this was the thinking that the oral transmission of the oral Torah was considered much more authentic than the written version.

CHAPTER III

An Overview of Christian Oral Tradition and Memorization in the Middle East

In this chapter we want to explore the subject of memorization of the Bible and liturgy in Christianity from the time of Jesus, through the Church Fathers, the Byzantine Period, the medieval and modern periods in the Church of the Middle East. We want to discover how the traditions of Jesus and the early Church were memorized and transmitted, and what level of importance was laid on the memorization and oral transmission of the Bible over the ages.

The Sayings of Jesus

We must start with the founder, Jesus of Nazareth. Between the words and works of Jesus and the earliest written records lies a period of diligent memorization of his teachings by his followers and their oral transmission. Biblical scholars have speculated about what may have happened during the time the disciples heard Jesus speak and when they transmitted his sayings to writing:

a. Those disciples who heard Jesus and talked about him wrote under the inspiration of the Holy Spirit without error.
b. Previously memorized short passages of the life and sayings of Jesus were recalled precisely and collected from others and set within recalled contexts.
c. The poetic stanzas in the Gospel records of Jesus' speech suggest that he taught in deliberate memorizable structures and spoke in memorable speech.
d. The presence of linking mnemonics similar to that in rabbinic Judaism.
e. A combination of all of the above.

Set aside the doctrine of inspiration momentarily and the 1st century followers of Jesus were like us in one respect; that they had a limited memory; they could retain up to a few words or connected phrases for about a minute. Then again if they had any kind of religious education they were likely somewhat skilled in the art of memorizing and familiar with the mnemonic techniques to carry out the transmission of the sayings of Jesus. So how were they able to memorize the sayings of Jesus and later transmit them to writing? The most utilized mnemonic tool in the oral world was verbal repetition. To achieve perfect recall after they heard Jesus speak, vast amounts of repetition were required. In repetition a memorized saying is recycled verbally and even internally, without alteration and can at some point be transferred intact to the long term memory. This memory is permanent in the sense that given sufficient effort the contents can be recalled verbatim at any time throughout the rest of one's life.[43] This might seem far fetched to many in the West, but I can testify to this phenomenon by personal experience. I have memorized numerous books of the Bible over the last few years and because of my continual repetition or meditating on them I can recall the entirety of these books verbatim at any given time with relative ease.

Jesus did speak in a way that facilitated memorization for his audience. Gleaning from the Gospels we can see that when Jesus taught he generally did so with the aid of short, artistically pointed sayings. These sayings were transmitted as memorized texts by his followers in the same techniques as Jewish parable-traditions. Some of the parables of Jesus contain features to foster memorization such as a preface, namely the stating of the topic first, as with *"The Kingdom of God is like..."* (Matthew 25). The unique authority of Jesus ensured the attention of his disciple while the use of different mnemonics aided their memorization later to write what they had memorized, the Gospels.[44] Jesus also structured some of his sermons such as the Sermon on the Mount on texts the audience likely had previously memorized. In doing so Jesus is making the message more attainable to retain by spacing out the key previously memorized texts throughout his message so the audience could then hang his words before and after their previously memorized texts quite easily. There were numerous other techniques Jesus used to facilitate the memorization of his words which will be discussed later. The conclusion of the matter is that the Jesus often taught in brief sayings and in memorizable forms to facilitate the memory of his followers and they then memorized his sayings verbatim via mnemonics and later faithfully transmitted his sayings verbatim to writing.

Memorized to the Written Gospel

There existed in the early church a traditional view of the origin of the oral and written transmission of the Gospels. That view is that all four Gospels derived from well known, reliable persons who stood at one or two persons removed from Jesus. This idea was expressed in passages as early as the 2nd century from Papias and Irenaeus and thereby influenced the views of the later Church Fathers. Those who memorized and transmitted the gospel were those who had been a personal disciple of Jesus; or someone who had followed a disciple of Jesus and personally heard him, and was therefore guaranteed to have memorized verbatim the words and works of Jesus. Like Judaism, an emphasis was placed in the early Church on the fact that the author in question was an eyewitness or that they bear witness to what they heard.[45]

The Church Fathers write that the Gospels were not originally crafted to be written down as a means of transmission but at first memorized and passed on orally. For example, Eusebius speaks in connection with the traditional view of the Gospels of Matthew and John being copied down only because of an emergency.[46] This once again reminds us of Judaism's reluctance to write down what is oral until an emergency arises. Interestingly Papias said that Matthew *"composed the sayings (of Jesus) in the Aramaic language."*[47] But Papias did not say Matthew "wrote" the Gospel as he does when speaking of Mark's Gospel, his word

43. John Bradshaw, *Expository Times vol. 92* pg. 303
44. Birger Gerhardsson, *The Gospel Tradition* pg. 39
45. Birger Gerhardsson, *Memory and Manuscript* pg. 194
46. Eusebius, *Hist. Eccl. III.24*
47. ibid *Hist. Eccl. III.39*

is "composed" a word that seems to be quite appropriate to what may be called oral composition.[48] The other references describe the way in which the evangelists eventually copied down that which they had memorized from hearing Jesus. Concerning the Gospel of Mark, Papias said he wrote down carefully what he memorized of Peter's oral teaching. John, who is said to have made use of the method of a memorized oral proclamation, published his Gospel at the end of his life only at the request of his friends.[49]

As for Luke's Gospel, the significance of the eyewitnesses of Jesus was not overlooked. In his prologue Luke identifies his sources and among them are *"the eyewitnesses and minister of the word"* (Luke 1:2). The single definite article suggests that the eyewitnesses and the ministers may be one in the same people. A *huperetes* (minister) was the leader of worship in a Greek speaking Jewish synagogue. Hebrew speaking synagogues had the same person who was and still is called a *hazzan*. This person also kept the scrolls of the synagogue and would be intimately acquainted with the Tenach. However, Luke described this early Christian official as a *huperetes* of the word not of the synagogue. Three elements are thus brought together to define this oral ministry. First the title for a worship leader in the synagogue is borrowed and reused. Secondly he must be an eyewitness and third he is a *hazzan* of the word of and about Jesus. So if you are an eyewitness, a leader in worship and a servant of the word of Jesus who are you? When these three elements are brought together it is fully possible to understand these special selected people as those designated to recite the traditions of and from Jesus by memory in worship and study sessions in the early Church. These designated memorizers of the tradition of Jesus passed their memorized recollections on to the early Christians and to Luke who then eventually wrote his Gospel.[50]

This understanding of how the oral tradition was passed on and preserved allows for the slight variations found in the written Gospels. It also guarantees authenticity for the oral material up to the composition of the written records. The need for authentic information about Jesus was profound. The earliest Christians were Jews who lived in an oral world and had committed themselves to Jesus as the Messiah. If they could not remember what he said and did, they could not preserve their own identity. Some of their material was likely memorized as the sayings of rabbi Jesus. Thus the methodologies of memorization in the rabbinic schools likely accounted for preserving the material of the Gospels. Also many of the sayings and works of Jesus were likely passed on in early Christian social settings or *samar's* (preserve) which continued accurately preserving the words of Jesus through the critical period of oral transmission. The breakup of settled Jewish village life caused by the first and second Jewish revolts against Rome would have disrupted this oral framework. But Christians who grew up between 30-70 CE with this tradition recited around them would be authentic witnesses to if for a lifetime even though they themselves were not eyewitnesses.[51] From the above mentioned we can conclude that the sayings of Jesus were wide spread in an oral fashion in the early Church in Israel via eyewitnesses and social settings, and from the testimonies of the Church Fathers we can presume that the original writing down of the Gospels was an emergency measure adopted for various reasons.

---

48. Edgar Goodspeed *An Introduction to the NT* pg. 129
49. Eusebius, *Hist. Eccl. VI. 14*
50. *Expository Times vol. 106* pg. 363
51. ibid pg. 367

Memorization and Orality in the Early Church

The sacred books of the Tenach and New Testament carried both the special authority of the written page and the living immediacy of oral reading and recitation from memory. The point emerges clearly in the New Testament, for example in the NRSV rendering of Revelation 1:3 we read: *"Blessed is the one who reads aloud the words of this prophecy."* Another indication of the necessity to orally proclaim only particular books is shown concerning a statement about the book, the Shepherd of Hermas which was to be read privately, but not publicly recited: *"therefore it must be indeed read, but cannot be publicly recited to the people in the church."*[52] Like Judaism, early Christianity stressed that what can be learned from the written page cannot be compared with that which may be learned from the lips of the living person.

It would seem that it was the task of the teachers in the early Church to teach this memorized oral Gospel to new converts as the Jewish *tanna* taught the oral Torah to their disciples. The greatest knowledge was to be found in oral teaching, in which the student memorized not only texts but also learned the interpretation. In the 2nd century Irenaeus spoke of the time when he had listened to Polycarp, relating what he himself had heard, not read, from John the apostle.[53] And Justin Martyr introduces the teachings of the gospels as "what Jesus said" and not as quotations from a book.[54]

Since we are not dealing with an illiterate society when we look at the New Testament world, we cannot take it for granted that there was likely a simple opposition between orality and literacy. However, even after literacy had been common, oral mentality and preference for orality seemed to persist. We should think in terms of a nuanced tension between orality and literacy, not a simple opposition since we are dealing with an ancient literate society where orality persisted. It was likely taken for granted that the written medium took a back seat to the oral medium. For example, an indication of Paul's initial reservation about writing can be detected in his references to his previous oral instruction in 1 Thessalonians. He may merely be referring back to his previous instruction given during his recent visit, but he seems to prefer face to face oral instruction than to a written medium.[55] According to Papias, the living voice was still the best medium for communication of Christian doctrine.[56]

Memorization and the Monastery in the Byzantine Period

Did the emphasis on memorization during the formative years of the Church transcend to the Byzantine Period monasteries? If so what level of importance was laid on memorization in the monastic world? Let us consider the monastic life in Egypt and Palestine.

Egypt

In the third and early fourth centuries we encounter a ceaseless monastic practice in Egypt of reciting the Psalms from memory. We are not sure when this practice began but we do know that this was the practice of such influential fathers as Antony and Palamon, Pachomius' teacher in the 3rd century. It was

52. William Graham, *Beyond the Written Word* pg. 220
53. Birger Gerhardsson, *Memory and Manuscript* pg. 197
54. Justin Martyr *1 Apology 15-17*
55. Akio Ito, *The Written Torah and the Oral Gospel* pg. 244
56. Eusebius, *Hist. Eccl. III. 39*

their practice to chant the Psalms from memory aloud throughout the whole day.[57] Let us consider the work of St. Pachomius, the founder of the most influential monastery in Egypt, who lived in the 4th century. The principal biographies tell us that as a young man he was a Roman soldier who converted to Christianity in 315. Some years after his conversion, he sought an anchorite life and with the help of his brother set up a monastery at Tabennesi in Upper Egypt. Here, under his leadership and guidance, and after him that of his two major disciples, Horsiesius and Theodore, a new kind of monastic community developed. Those Christians who sought refuge in the Byzantine period came together in huge numbers to the discipline and Rule of the Pachomian community. Pachomius formed first one, then a number of monastic communities in Egypt. When Pachomius died in 346, he left behind a large number of monasteries teeming with formidable communities, and his system of monastic life spread to many of the other monastic centers all over the Middle East. One modest record states that the Pachomian foundation in Tabennesis housed 7,000 monks, Mount Nitrea 5,000, and Arsinoe over 10,000.[58]

The lines of continuity that connected the Pachomian community and their Rule and later Christian monastic institutions are clearly evident. The spread of the Pachomian Rule was evident first in the East. It took hold early in Ethiopia, and reached Mesopotamia and Persia in the 4th century.[59] As late as the 12th century a Pachomian monastery was functioning in Constantinople. Pachomian influence filtered into the West by several literary routes: Athanasius, Jerome, and John Cassian in the 4th century. Pachomian monasticism was a significant model for as well as a temporal precursor of later Christian monastic practice. Let us consider some of the Church leaders who were influenced by the Pachomian rule. St. John Chrysostom bishop of Constantinople stayed under the Pachomian rule in the Thebaid from 373 to 381. St. Jerome (342-420) and Rufinus (345-410), the ecclesiastical historian, came from Italy and spent time with the community. St. Basil (330-379), the Cappadocian Father introduced monasticism into Byzantium on the basis of his Pachomian apprenticeship. St. John Cassian (360-435) passed seven years in the Thebaid and the Nitrean desert before introducing monasticism into Gaul.[60] Whatever emphasis was laid on memorization by the Pachomian Rule and community was surely to be found in a similar manner at other sister monasteries and in the habits of those Church Fathers who were at one time under the Pachomian Rule.

The founder Pachomius gave himself up to memorizing and reciting aloud books of Scripture. He had his heart set on reciting them in order and with great ease.[61] So it is no surprise that we find in the Pachomian Rule a tremendous emphasis on memorizing the Bible. What would it have been like to join the monastery and what emphasis on memorization would they place on the novice? Part of the Rules of Pachomius deals with the reception of the novice monk: *"Whoever enters the monastery uninstructed shall be taught first what he must observe; and when, so taught, he has consented to it all, they shall give him twenty Psalms or two of the Apostle's epistles, or some other part of the Scripture (to memorize)."*[62] And in another place it is written: *"There shall be no one whatever in the monastery who does not learn to read and does not memorize*

---

57. Joseph Patrich, *Sabas, Leader of Palestinian Monasticism* pg. 230
58. Aziz Atiya, *A History of Eastern Christianity* pg. 63
59. William Graham, *Beyond the Written Word* pg. 128
60. Aziz Atiya, *A History of Eastern Christianity* pg. 65
61. *Pachomian Koinonia* 1:38
62. ibid 2:166

something of the Scriptures. One should learn by heart at least the New Testament and the Psalter."[63] The very first prerequisite for entry into and participation in the monastery was memorization of a minimum amount of Scripture. All of the Byzantine monasteries under the Pachomian Rule were united by the ties of a common practice of memorizing massive portions of the Bible.

Just how important knowing the Scriptures by heart was in the context of the monastic life is difficult for most to grasp in the 21st century printed world. Memorizing the Scriptures was and should be today the first step to realizing its guidance and protection in one's life and actions as well as one's speech. On this note Pachomius said to his monks: *"If then an impure thought rises up in your heart or hatred…and if you want all these thoughts to diminish in you and not to have power over you, then recite in your heart without ceasing every fruit that is written in the Scriptures."*[64] Memorization provided the first line of access to the Scriptures, and it was an access that allowed for recitation of Scripture at the numerous times in a day when reading a Bible was not possible. It was this immediate accessibility of the memorized Bible of which Theodore, the disciple of Pachomius speaks: *"Now then, my brothers, I assure you before God and his Christ that a single (memorized) Psalm is possibly enough to save us if we understand it well, act on it, and observe it. But above all, we have always at hand the Gospels of our Lord Jesus Christ and all the rest of the Holy Scriptures and their thoughts."*[65] The monks were expected to be able immediately to call up the words of the Bible hid in their heart so they might act on those verses and not sin against God.

If we could go back in time we would have found that very little went on in monastic life without the accompaniment of the memorization and recitation from Scripture. There was an intensity of the preoccupation with the divine word. We find substantial references to memorization of Scripture; to recitation as a major preoccupation in its own right; to liturgical recitation, to the chanting of Scripture while walking, weaving, baking, and greeting visitors; and to Scripture recitation during the communal meals and as the basis of all teaching and preaching in the monastic community which we will discuss in greater detail later.[66] Everything revolved around the memorization of the Scriptures. The necessities of Pachomius and the thousands of monasteries his Rule influenced for both reading aloud and recitation of the Scriptures from memory were as explicit as they were fundamental. As we shall later see the previously mentioned Church Fathers who were influenced by Pachomian rule and practice, preached to their flock and wrote extensively on the spiritual benefits of memorizing Scripture.

Palestine

Let us make our way out of Egypt and consider the importance of memorization in the monastic world of Palestine in the Byzantine period. Just as we saw in Egypt, memorization of the book of Psalms was one of the basic requirements for a monastic life in Palestine and was not just for your average monk but for those who were also youths. Sabas in the 5th century had already learned all the Psalms from memory by the age of eight when he started out in the Flaviana monastery in Cappadocia. Sabas, during the eleven years that he lived in the coenbium of Theoctistus would spend his days in physical labor and his nights without

---

63. ibid 2:166
64. ibid 1:453
65. ibid 1:231
66. William Graham, *Beyond the Written Word* pg. 131

sleep reciting all the Psalms from memory. The story of Sabas and the lion in a cave near the river of Gadara informs us about the practice of the anchorite in the recitation of the night Psalms. The lion, in whose cave Sabas established as his dwelling, returned to the cave and found Sabas sleeping. Sabas arose apparently unalarmed by the lion, completed the recitation of the Psalms and went back to sleep.[67] The night that a pillar of fire pointed out to him the location of the cave in which he established the Theoktistos Church, he was wandering along the Kidron Valley reciting the Psalms.[68] Sabas like Pachomius demanded the memorization of the Psalms from the novices who came to him at the laura.[69]

Theodosius also in the 5th century as a child served as a reader in the church of Comana in Cappadocia where he learned by heart the book of Psalms and other Scriptures.[70] He was so devoted to the memorization of the Psalms that even on his deathbed he took care to appoint in each of the churches he founded the monks who would chant the Psalms from memory. About the same time, Palladius wrote about an ascetic monk named Adolius who lived on the Mount of Olives and his devotion to memorization. From the evening until the vigil prayer he would stand outside reciting the Psalms from memory. When the time for the service began he would pass between the cells and bang with a clapper on the doors, awakening the monks for the night prayer. It was only when this was finished before dawn that he would hasten to his cell for a short rest, until the next time of reciting the Psalms which began with sunrise.[71] Palladius also wrote of a monk named Elpidius who would recite the Psalms from memory at night standing and continued this practice for twenty-five years.[72]

In the 6th century laura of Chariton the monks not only recited Psalms from memory at prayer times, but did so while working in their cell on craftwork.[73] Around the same time John Moschus also tells of a monk reciting Psalms in his cell while engaged in basket weaving and other monks reciting Psalms during the course of the day.[74] John also informs us that certain Psalms were said from heart at certain times of the day. He mentions the Psalms of the third hour recited by an anchorite who lived in a cave near the Jordan River.[75] The importance of memorization in the Palestinian monastery was deeply influenced by the Rule of Pachomius in Upper Egypt during the 4th century. As in Egypt nothing went out in the daily life of the monk in Palestine without the memorization and constant recitation of the memorized Bible.

Memorization in the Byzantine Period

In this section I would like to discuss the memorization of persons within the different denominations of the Middle Eastern Church of the Byzantine period that were not previously covered. Though primary sources on the subject are difficult to come by I trust what I have found would be sufficient to give us a feeling of their take on memorization of the Bible and liturgy.

---

67. Joseph Patrich *Sabas, Leader of Palestinian Monasticism* pg. 235
68. Joseph Patrich *Sabas, Leader of Palestinian Monasticism* pg. 236
69. ibid pg. 229
70. ibid pg. 230
71. ibid pg. 231
72. ibid pg. 236
73. ibid pg. 232
74. ibid pg. 232
75. ibid pg. 233

Copts

There was and still is a tremendous emphasis on memorization of the Bible and liturgy within Coptic circles. Let us trace important documents or persons in their tradition which emphasized memorization. Our knowledge of Coptic biblical literature is very limited. The place of the Copts in the general history of Christianity has been minimized, sometimes even forgotten, partly because the Coptic people themselves had voluntarily chosen to live in oblivion.[76] Therefore we have little textual evidence to inform us on their emphasis on memorization. We do know the Catechetical School of Alexandria was one of the earliest institutions of theological learning in Christian antiquity. Its members were responsible for the formulation of the first systems of Christian theology and for some of the most monumental works of exegesis. We do have quotes from some of the school's major thinkers on memorization which would infer the trickle down effect it had on those under their authority.

Let us start with the founder of the church in Egypt, Mark the evangelist. Clement of Alexandria said that Peter's hearers exhorted Mark, as one who had long been a follower of Peter and had memorized his teaching, to write down what Peter had said.[77] We know that Mark spent time teaching and doing missionary work in Egypt in the 1st century and it is plausible that Mark instructed his students in an oral fashion, communicating to them what he had previously memorized from Peter and others of the words and works of Jesus. Clement of Alexandria in the 2nd century still lived in an oral world, and struggled with the notion of putting down in writing his work *Stromateis*. Yet, Clement had come to the conclusion that now was the time when oral tradition should be written down. Much had been forgotten and unless what he now remembered was written all may have been lost. Elsewhere he says: *"For the sacred trust of the elders speaks through writing and uses the help of the writer for the handing down of tradition for the salvation of those who will read it."*[78] At this critical stage Clement felt himself to be the link between the apostolic past and the Church of the future and it was this emergency that prompted him to write down.

Athanasius became the patriarch of Alexandria in the 4th century. An interesting account tells of the monks of Pachomius reception of the archbishop Athanasius, on occasions when he visited Upper Egypt: *"Apa Theodore and his brothers went north. They found the archbishop in the northern part of the diocese of Shmoun. He was mounted on a donkey and countless people were following him...chanting Psalms and canticles. Apa Theodore quickly put into shore in front of the monasteries of the diocese of Shmoun. He took with him, too, all the brothers of those monasteries and, reciting all together from the words of the Scriptures and the Gospels of our Lord Jesus Christ, they went north on foot to meet him."*[79] St. Athanasius also encouraged the oral participation of the audience in the service with the readings of the Psalms. Such an oral exercise as we will later see fostered memorization of the antiphonal text. St. Athanasius: *"urged his deacon to read a Psalm and the people to respond: For his mercy endures forever"* (Psalm 136).[80]

St. Cyril (412-444) followed Athanasius as Patriarch. Following an early Church custom, Cyril composed many sermons which he sent to all the bishops of Greece, who, in turn, memorized them and preached them

---

76. Aziz Atiya, *A History of Eastern Christianity* pg. 13
77. Eusebius, *Hist. Eccl. VI. 14*
78. Clement, *Ecl. Propoh. 27.4*
79. William Graham, *Beyond the Written Word* pg. 137
80. Harold W. Attridge, *Psalms in Community* pg. 19

to their own congregations.[81] We have very little textual evidence to inform us of the role of memorization in the Coptic world but what we do have points towards a high view of memorization in an orally dominant world.

Armenians

The history concerning the Armenian Church is well known but what role memorization played during the Byzantine period is not. That the monks would certainly know the Psalms from memory as we will later see was a common phenomenon in monastic circles in the Byzantine period. Also the liturgies of St. Chrysostom and St. Basil were likely memorized from their constant readings in the services. I asked Father Kousan of the Armenian Church in Jerusalem if he knew of anyone from this period that was especially known for memorizing or of any sources that would shed light on the subject and he said: *"I don't know of any individuals in our Church history who stand out as memorizers."* He went on to say: *"I know of many Protestants who memorize but in our community I have never met anyone who emphasized this exercise or was especially gifted in memorization, except an 80 year old man I know."* This is not to say that there were not memorizers, the surrounding monastic communities in Palestine certainly memorized Scripture and liturgy as we will see and it is likely the same situation existed in the Armenian Church.

Syrians

Ephrem the Syrian was the foremost writer in the Syriac tradition of Christianity and was the first Syrian theologian to put commentary in poetical form. He was born in Nisibis near the beginning of the 4th century and spent his early life there, teaching and writing hymns, homilies and commentaries. Ephrem later continued his rich literary production in Edessa, where he established both a school of biblical and theological studies and women's choirs to sing his hymns.[82] Ephrem's importance for the history of Syrian literature and for the history of Christianity in the Syriac-speaking context is immense. His hymns have remained central in both the East and West Syrian liturgical traditions. The hymnic forms that he used became the standard forms of all subsequent Syriac literature and made the songs easier to memorize because of their poetic form. Appreciation of Ephrem's hymns was not limited to those who just spoke Syriac. Among the Eastern traditions most closely allied with the Syriac- Greek, Coptic, Ethiopic, and Armenian, Ephrem found a place almost as central as in his own tradition.[83] Is there any evidence from Ephrem's hymns that he constructed them in a way to be memorized? Let us consider just the opening stanzas of his third poem from *The Hymns on the Nativity:*

Section 1

> *Blessed be the Child…*
> *Blessed be the Newborn…*
> *Blessed be the Fruit…*
> *Blessed be the Gracious One…*
> *Blessed be He…*

81. Mary Carruthers, *The Book of Memory* pg. 159
82. Kathleen McVey, *Ephrem the Syrian* pg. 3
83. ibid pg. 4

Section 2

Thanks to the Fountainhead…

Thanks to the One who…

Thanks to the One who…

Thanks to the Compassionate One…

Sections 3-5

Glory to that One Who…

Glory to the Silent One…

Glory to that Sublime One…

Glory to the Spiritual One…

Glory to that Hidden One…

Glory to that Living One…

Glory to that Great One…

Glory to that One Power…

Glory to that Hidden One…

Sections 6-7 all start with:

Blessed is He…

Sections 8-9:

Glory to the Son

Glory to the One

Glory to the Beautiful One

Glory to the Serene One

Glory to the Heavenly One

As you can see by reading just the opening lines of each stanza it was constructed in a repetition form by Ephrem to facilitate memorization. This is just one example of the many hymns written by Ephrem that contain built in mnemonic devices to assist those who heard and read his liturgy to memorize it.

Let us also consider the memorization of the Psalms among the Syrians. In the 4th century community of Juliana Saba, the monks would assemble for communal vespers that included the reciting of the Psalms from memory. During the day, however, the disciples would walk in pairs in the desert and recite from memory in turn fifteen Psalms in succession from the early morning to the late afternoon.[84] Around the same time in the monastery of Publius in Zeugma all the members of the community met for the chanting of memorized Psalms in the morning and in the evening.[85] As we see the religious importance and edification of memorizing and reciting the Psalms was also found in Syria.

Ethiopians

The book of Psalms has from the very birth of Christianity has been the backbone of Christian prayer. It is especially the Ethiopians which have used the memorized Psalms in their liturgical services. The divine

---

84. Joseph Patrich *Sabas, Leader of Palestinian Monasticism* pg. 232

85. ibid pg. 232

office sung in these services is traditionally divided into seven hours, according to the verse: *"Seven times a day do I praise thee"* (Psalm 119: 164). In private devotionals, Ethiopian Christians traditionally recite the entire book of Psalms weekly in the following order: Monday 1-30, Tuesday 31-60, Wednesday 61-80, Thursday 81-110, Friday 111-130, Saturday 131-150, and on Sunday the Cantica of the Old and New Testament.[86] In private prayer the Psalms are widely used by all Christians in Ethiopia, to such a degree that the expression "to repeat or recite David" has come to mean the act of praying in general. In order to get a first hand opinion upon the importance of orality and memorization in the Ethiopian Church I interviewed a former member and now Protestant from Ethiopia at the Church of the Holy Sepluchre. I asked him if he could tell me about the importance of memorizing in the Ethiopian religious school: *"I was brought up in an oral world, in the Ethiopian School. We were told to memorize the book of Dawid by oral transmission; there were very few books at our disposal. Everything in the school was taught via oral transmission."* This statement agrees whole heartedly with Dr. Pedersen's statements in her book on Ethiopian exegesis.

Greek Orthodox

The 4th century text *Apostolic Tradition* refers to the liturgical use of the Psalms with oral responses by the congregation: *"They shall rise, then after supper and pray; and the boys and the virgins shall say Psalms (from memory). And then the deacon, when he receives the mixed cup of the offering, shall say a Psalm from those in which "Alleluia" is written, and then, if the priest so directs, again from the same Psalms. And after the bishop has offered the cup, he shall say the whole of a Psalm which applies to the cup, with "Alleluia" all joining in."*[87] The practice of gathering to sing Psalms appropriate to the hour, found in the above mentioned 4th century text, is still maintained today by the Greek Orthodox Liturgy of the Hours. I witnessed this oral phenomenon while I stayed with the monks at Mar Sabas monastery in 2009. Responsorial psalmody consists in the congregation repeating a Psalm verse or short exclamation such as "Alleluia" after each segment or verse of the Psalm spoken by the cantor. I must have heard "Alleluia" said fifty times during the midnight service. The psalmody opens with the cantor proclaiming in the response, thus instructing the people, who did not have books with them in ancient times but do today. I observed that some of the monks did not even have to have the Bible or the liturgical books open during the service because they have the majority of it memorized. Though some of the monks who were not as fluent in Greek held a candle to read the text inside the Theoktistos Church with has no electricity. Yet I did notice the cantor always read from the text though he likely had it memorized. The congregation repeats the response after the cantor, who then proceeds to proclaim the Psalm verses one by one, with the people repeating the response after each.[88] In the Byzantine rite the entire Psalter is read continually once a week, and twice a week during Lent.[89] This oral interplay between the cantor and the congregation fosters memorization for the audience by the necessity to play close attention to the antiphonal liturgy and the oral and aural demands the service puts on the participant. It was not only Psalms that were memorized but also hymns. Beginning in the 7th century, the churches of Jerusalem and the monastery of Mar Sabas fostered the composition of hymns for

86. Kirsten Stoffregen Pedersen, *Traditional Ethiopian Exegesis of the Book of Psalms*, pg. 13
87. Harold W. Attridge, *Psalms in Community* pg. 19
88. ibid pg. 17
89. Kirsten Stoffregen Pedersen, *Traditional Ethiopian Exegesis of the Book of Psalms*, pg. 11

use between the Psalms and canticles of the Book of the Hours. Initially limited to Sunday and feasts, the replacement of the old antiphonal refrains with melodious exegeses of theology by Sophronios of Jerusalem and John of Damascus proved to be enormously popular.[90]

Latins

The Latin rite secured the reading of the entire Psalter every week in its services until the last century. This exercise of hearing and reading all 150 Psalms from memory every week would have certainly made the memorization of them more attainable. The *Breviarium Romanum* until the reform of Pius X in 1911 was the simplest Latin form: twelve Psalms everyday in the early morning service, running from Psalms 1-110. Five Psalms were recited daily at vespers taken from 109-147. At *laudes* the same Psalms were always recited: 50, 62, 66, 148-150. The reform brought about by the II Vatican Council in the early 1960's has now distributed the Psalms over four weeks instead of the ancient practice of once a week.[91] This redistribution of the reading of the Psalms concurs with the statement made by Father Matthew in Jerusalem: *"we do not memorize the Bible in this age, though in ages past there was an emphasis placed upon it in the Church."*

Memorization in the Medieval Period

During the medieval period the oral role of Scripture took precedence over the written and memorization was still emphasized as religiously edifying even though the world began to become more written. Illiteracy was likely high among the masses of the Christian laity during this period and even literate Christians probably had limited opportunity for living with a Bible. Nevertheless, reading was still essentially an oral activity.[92] During this period many still read with their lips, pronouncing what they saw, and with the ears, listening to the words pronounced and hearing what is called the "voices of the pages."[93] This was done in order to pronounce the sacred words in order to memorize them; both the audible reading and the exercise of memory and meditation which it precedes were involved. To meditate is to read the text and to learn it by heart in the fullest sense, with one's whole being: with the body, since the mouth pronounced it, with the memory which fixes it, with the intelligence which understands its meaning and with the will which desires to put in into practice.[94] This resulted in more than a visual memory of the written words of the Bible but a muscular memory of the mouth and an aural memory of the words heard. The meditation consists in applying oneself with attention to this exercise in total memorization.

Memorization of the vernacular of the Bible was commonplace for the great figures of the Reformation and subsequent Protestantism. Though they are outside of our study in the Middle East I still think it noteworthy to mention their emphasis placed upon memorization. It is remarkable how completely a Martin Luther, John Calvin, or John Bunyan speaks in scripturally saturated language, that is, thinks, speaks, and writes in the vocabulary, modes, and imagery of the memorized Bible. In fact John Calvin developed a rhymed version of the book of Psalms to assure they could be easily sung and thereby memorized by the

90. Harold W. Attridge, *Psalms in Community* pg. 344
91. Kirsten Stoffregen Pedersen, *Traditional Ethiopian Exegesis of the Book of Psalms,* pg. 13
92. William Graham, *Beyond the Written Word* pg. 141
93. Jean Leclercq, *The Love of Learning and the Desire for God* pg. 19
94. ibid pg. 22

congregation.[95] Such persons do not so much quote Scripture or use it for proof texting as they simply speak Scripture, a Scripture they can and did recite by heart.[96] Martin Luther's aural sense of the Bible was in one respect grounded in his own practical experience and that of his age. Knowing Scripture by heart was something assumed for the serious theologian. Luther recognized clearly the importance of memorizing and retaining the Bible. He believed that Scripture should not only be heard, but *"also learned (memorized) and retained."* He himself had memorized Scripture in the Latin of the Vulgate and thus could remark: *"then I ran through the Scriptures as I had them in memory."* To the Christian then and today Luther says: *"You should meditate. That is, always repeat the oral speech and the literal word in the Bible and compare them with each another, not only in your heart, but also outwardly."*[97] Even though we are in the milieu of a written world there was still an emphatic emphasis on the necessity of memorizing and reciting the Bible.

Memorization in the Modern Period

Before we investigate what level of importance is laid on memorization today in the Church of the Middle East I must indicate that the primary source of our information is not from written texts but from living persons in the Church. In my opinion this is much better and follows after the early Christian and Judaic practice that what can be learned and memorized from a still book cannot be compared with what can be learned from the living person. As I have interviewed many persons from the many different denominations I have found that the general consensus today is that there is not an emphasis on memorization like there was in all the previous periods. That is not to say there are not certain individuals within the different denominations who do consider memorization as religiously edifying and a necessity in their daily walk. The emphasis today seems to be more geared towards knowing the liturgy from heart than the Bible and a reliance on the written text and not the memory. The vast majority of those interviewed have communicated to me that memorization comes by default of the continual oral and aural repetition of the Bible and liturgy heard in their daily services. There are some though who seemed more emphatic about memorization than others such as the Copts. The Copts displayed to me there amazing memorization skills by almost effortlessly speaking large portions of their liturgy from memory. Yet, I am convinced from eyewitness testimonies that they are in the minority in our written world. I had not found one monk today among all the denominations who for example knew all the Psalms from memory or could quote an entire Gospel like we read was common place in the early monastic movements in Egypt. Memorization has been essentially placed on the back burner with primarily only a reliability on the printed book. Such statements as *"There is no need to memorize today because we have the accessibility of books"* by Father Gomidass Sherbetdjianan of the Armenian Church and *"As a general rule we don't stress memorization but rely on reading the written word"* by Abu Shimon of the Syrian Church, and *"In my experience there is not an importance laid on memorization at any level in the Greek Orthodox Church from the seminary to the monastery,"* by Father Ioannes of the Greek Orthodox, and *"There is very little direct emphasis on memorization, especially on Scripture"* by Father Matthew of the Latin rite, lead me to the understanding that memorization is becoming more and more scarce in the 21st century printed world which the Church finds itself in the midst of.

95. Kirsten Stoffregen Pedersen, *Traditional Ethiopian Exegesis of the Book of Psalms*, pg. 13
96. William Graham, *Beyond the Written Word* pg. 144
97. William Graham, *Beyond the Written Word* pg. 149

Conclusion

The relationship to the memorized word of the text is inherently dynamic and personal in a way that the relationship to the printed word alone is not. The oral dimension was intimately bound up with the major personal and communal roles of Scripture in religious life, especially those that moved not only in the intellectual realm, but also in the sense of ritual and devotional use. The spoken word has been the most important medium through which religious persons and groups throughout history have known and interacted with Scriptural texts.[98] To understand the phenomenon of Scripture in any fashion we must look to its function as a text that above all has been read and recited aloud, repeated and memorized, chanted and sung in the oral world of daily life. The very act of learning a text by heart internalized that text in a way that familiarity with even an often read text does not. Memorization is a particularly intimate appropriation of a text, and the capacity to quote a text from memory is a spiritual resource that is tapped automatically in every act of reflection, worship, prayer, or moral deliberation. Oral mastery of Scripture was the ideal form of scriptural piety.[99] It is a vastly different thing to read and revere a text as an authoritative document than to internalize it in memory and meditation until it permeates the sensual as well as the intellectual sphere of consciousness. This internalization, leads the person of faith to accept the guidance of the text that its word becomes effectively absolute. The Church in the West and I perceive now partially in the East is out of the ordinary in its understanding of the orality of the memorized Scripture, largely because of its loss of a significant oral relationship to the Bible and their generally dismal attitude towards memorizing the Bible.

---

98. ibid pg. 155
99. ibid pg. 160

CHAPTER IV

Who Memorized in Judaism?

In this chapter we want to point out different individuals and institutions that memorized the Bible and rabbinic literature over the history of Judaism. In doing so I hope to highlight the necessity put on memorization by that niche of the populace at different periods of time. Even when the Jewish people were not immersed in an oral world, the broad masses have always been more persuadable to the appeal of oral proclamation than to a written version. In fact, all great religious movements in Judaism were popular oral movements. The memorized oral proclamations were the volcanic eruptions of human passions and emotions, stirred into activity by the torch of the spoken word cast into the midst of the people. It is these memorizers who lit such a burning fire under the Jewish people and spurred them on to piety and reform.

The Storyteller in the Biblical Period

What was the role of the storyteller in the biblical period and what place did memorization have in their oral performance? Unfortunately the ancient history of the Jewish storyteller is shrouded in obscurity. Our only source for this person is the best source, the Bible, but only a few small details can cast light on the subject. In biblical times there must have been expert storytellers who specialized in recounting the annals of Israel, but we know little about such people. These popular story tellers, familiar with Bible songs and stories, likely wandered about the country and were to be found for hire, or in the king's palace, and in the open air at market places and popular feasts. A good case can be made that stories such as Ruth were handed down by memory, in the elevated prose style which we have in the written transmission, and were originally composed in an oral style and told by such people. Differences of performance between one story and another would be due to the individual creativity of the story tellers, each of whom could likely recite many famous stories from the Bible. Some have suggested that the identity of the itinerant speakers in the time of Josiah were the Levites who had the task of going around the country teaching and explaining the Torah.[100] All that being said, we really don't know much if anything about these ancient performers. But we can use modern day reflections from the Middle East that can help paint a picture of what a story telling session might have looked like long ago. For example, let us consider the modern day Bedouin storyteller as a window into this oral world. I stayed with the Bedouin in Wadi Rum in Jordan for a short time and during one evening the time came for the evening entertainment. In the midst of a desert ocean, half a dozen Bedouin men arose from around the camp fire and from memory sang Bedouin folk songs, tales, and *suras* of the Koran. They sang such oral literature from heart with ease and in complete unison with one another without the aid of music. One can readily imagine how easy it could be as an audience member after hearing such rhythmic melodies even a few times to memorize what the men were singing. I think that this example

---

100. Yitzhak Buxbaum, *Storytelling and Spirituality in Judaism* pg. 6

is a window of what could have been expected of an ancient Israelite storyteller in this conservative and slow paced region of the world.

The Poet in the Biblical Period

The oral poet though similar in function to the storyteller had a different role in ancient Israelite society. Like the storyteller we know little about the role of the oral poet and our information comes from inferences from the Bible alone. The oral poet was one who often transmitted and composed poetry without the aid of writing, and reproduced their poems on demand with the aid of a fixed vocabulary and a powerful and highly trained memory.

We can imagine David shepherding the flock in the Judean wilderness and through his real life experiences composing Psalm 23, or lying under an olive tree on the outskirts of Bethlehem in the night and looking up to the heavens and composing Psalm 8 and then singing these songs to an audience who would memorize them. Due to lack of evidence, especially at the sociological level, much of the surmise concerning oral elements in ancient Hebrew poetry must remain conjecture. We know very little about the oral performer (for instance, questions about their identity, training, pay, special literary forms preferred all remain unanswerable) or about their social position, the behavior of the audience, where and when the performances took place and so on. We do know that the poets along with the scribes were the custodians of tradition. Their art was an expression of the life of the Jewish community. Their narratives and poems were filled with ideas and theologies characteristic not only of the soul of the author, but of the geographical and cultural surroundings in which they lived. The religious works of the people, their poetry, and stories of their heroes were maintained by these poets, who had learned their craft, their stories and their way of telling them, from their elders, and practiced it in much the same way to the next generation.[101]

The Scribe in the Biblical Period

Unless one wanted to read a scroll from beginning to end in one or a series of sittings, the scroll was cumbersome as a handy source of information. The most effective use of the scroll for information retrieval was available only to scribes themselves who had access to one, and were so familiar with the text that they would know where to find what they needed. The text was as much a fact of their memory as it was a physical object. The primary function of a scribe is that of one whose work consisted in transcribing a text by his own hand. The scribe may perform his professional work in many ways. He may preferably copy out his text by eye having beside him the authoritative text to be transcribed. This method relies on the purely visual medium and the regular split-second effort of memory with or without oral repetition of what he is transcribing. On the other hand, the scribe may transcribe his text from dictation like Baruch the scribe of Jeremiah (Jeremiah 36). This method relies on the purely aural medium and aural memory with perhaps again some oral repetition of what has just been read to him for transcription. Or, as a third way, he may transcribe his text is from memory, we see a later example of this in rabbinic Judaism when R. Meir copied the book of Esther from memory while in Ephesus (b. Meg 18b), though as we previously read the strictest

---

101. *The Catholic Biblical Quarterly vol. 23* pg. 405

rules governed the copying of the Torah in the Second Temple period.[102] Well educated scribes could likely write out a verbatim, memorized form of an authoritative text. We have examples of this which we will see later in the rabbinic period (b. Meg. 18b).

Everyday People in the Biblical Period

In general it can be assumed that the audiences were not mere passive spectators to an oral enactment, but joined in actively when a story teller or poet spoke a familiar account. We see this even today, and have to wonder how far back the audience's verbal reaction at the name of Haman in the oral rendition of the book of Esther during Purim has gone on. Of such activities we can glean a few hints from the Bible. Refrains and questions from the Psalms show that the people listening were not always mute; for example: *"Who is the King of Glory?"* and someone would respond, *"The Lord of Hosts he is the king of glory"* (Psalm 24). And the phrase *"For his mercy endures forever"* is repeated by the audience after each of the 26 stanzas in Psalm 136. This particular Psalm was designed to be directed by a Levitical choir instructor with the audience chiming in from memory at the second stanza of every verse. This Psalm was sung in the Temple of Solomon on the day of its dedication (2 Chronicles 7:3), and was also sung four generations later by the singers appointed by Jehoshaphat who went ahead of the troops to battle in the Judean wilderness (2 Chr. 20:21).[103] The oral interplay between the director and the audience likely helped to foster memorization and preserve these Psalms to the next generation.

Social Settings in the Biblical Period

The term social setting includes not only a particular community activity, like preaching, but also cultural characteristics of the community, for example, how texts were used generally throughout the culture. Broadly speaking, at least three main classes of occasion can be identified where stories and songs would be sung in ancient Israel: family affairs, inter tribal occasions such as feasts and liturgical festivals and informal social gatherings.[104] Let me explain; before and after birth there were oracles spoken (Genesis 25:23, Isaiah 11:1-9), and explanations of names given (Genesis 18). Coming of age was marked by an oral blessing (Genesis 27:27) and marriage was an excuse for a feast at which songs were sung and riddle contests held (Judges 14:12-18). At death a final blessing could be in poetic form (Genesis 49) and there were often funeral chants (Jeremiah 22:18). Songs were also sung from heart at work: while digging a well (Numbers 21:17), harvesting (Isaiah 16:10), or guarding the city (Isaiah 21:11). The Jews streaming to Jerusalem from all over the land would sing traditional songs from memory such as the Psalms of Ascent (120-134). We can also imagine an informal setting like a social gathering of a community. People would come expecting to listen to and recite the tradition of the community. This kind of gathering is called in Hebrew *samar* (preserve). The community would gather to preserve its store of historical recollections and inherited wisdom. Nothing would be concretely planned. There is no designated story teller, nor any guild of story tellers who alone are allowed to speak. With some limits young and old, male and female, who know how to tell the story the correct way can recite. Yet what is happening is considered serious and deemed important enough though

---

102. Martin S. Jaffee, *Torah in the Mouth* pg. 17
103. Wilfred Watson, *Classical Hebrew Poetry, A Guide to its Techniques* pg. 78
104. ibid pg. 79

the setting is informal.[105] In the orally dominant environment of the biblical period almost every aspect of life from birth to marriage to death, was integrated into the memory by phrasing or singing such accounts in a memorable way.

The Storyteller in the Rabbinic Period

Telling and retelling stories was also a favored oral characteristic in the rabbinic period. The temptation today in talking about the meaning of a story is to summarize what happened in it, or to tell what values it affirms, thereby reducing the storytelling to a communication device instead of letting the words of the story speak for themselves and trusting that the audience is intelligent enough to grasp its content. One only needs to read a few pages in the Talmud to see how fundamental storytelling was in instructing the Jews in *halacha*. There was not a reason to summarize the main points of the story to the listener but let the story speak and teach on its own two legs.

The Scribe in the Rabbinic Period

Many of the scribes during the rabbinic period were like those in ancient Israel, that is to say they could speak and write out the whole Bible from heart. Not all scribes had, like R. Huna copied the entire Torah 70 times (b. Batra 14a), or like R. Ishmael ben Jose or R. Hiyya who knew the text so well that they could *"write out the whole of Scriptures from memory"* (b. Meg. 18b). But despite their extraordinary capacity for memorizing, rabbinic Judaism had an emphatically repeated rule that the written Torah was not to be copied out from memory in order to safe guard the transmission of the text. Of course there are exceptions to every rule. We read that R. Meir, while in Ephesus on finding out that a Hebrew scroll of the book of Esther was missing was compelled to write the complete book from memory just in time to be able to read from the book at the Purim festival (b Meg. 18b). This is not to say that rabbinic Judaism did not encourage memorization of the Bible, we have numerous examples in the Talmud of young men training in the academy being quizzed on the memory verses (b. Hulin 95b, b. Git. 56a). The copyist who wanted to transmit the written Torah according to *halacah* had to have a written edition before him. Not a single letter might be copied without having the text before one's eyes (b. Meg. 18b).[106] As we saw from R. Ishmael ben Jose and R. Hiyya it is probable that numerous scribes during the rabbinic period had the whole of Scriptures memorized because of their copying out the Tenach so many times.

The Rabbi in the Rabbinic Period

The deliberate use of memorizing that we earlier saw in the first century CE gave the Hebrew language and its forms of expression some highly individual characteristics. Since many of the texts that were learnt by heart were taken from the oral and written Torah, the learner's mind was stored with biblical and *halacha* facts, sentences and figures, which explains the innumerable echoes that were likely to be heard in the speech of the Jewish people at that time. The teachers of Judaism wishing both to help the memory and to imprint the learning that it was to retain and transmit as deeply as possible, had devised a whole system of

---

105. *Expository Times vol. 106* pg. 364
106. Birger Gerhardsson, *Memory and Manuscript* pg. 46

mnemonics; rhythms, melodies, alliterations, repetitions of words and antitheses which made the recollection of the verbal elements easier throughout the rabbinic period.[107] I list numerous techniques that were used to memorize in Judaism later in the book. The rabbis were well aware that memorization could be facilitated by a technique: sometimes simple, sometimes advanced. The experiences and observations of centuries of memorization had produced real results. When we come to the time the Talmud was closed in the 6th century, we find a technique of mnemonics which had developed enormously. These mnemonic features were the nuts and bolts that facilitated memorization for the rabbis. Some rabbis receive special mention for their extraordinary ability to memorize. R. Judah b. Ilai is particularly noted among the Tannaites; R. Nahman b. Issac, and R. Judah b. Hanina among the Amoraic rabbis. This is not to say that they were the only rabbis who were mindful of the process of mnemonic techniques. That they are singled out for special mention is evidently due to the fact that they distinguished themselves from other rabbis by laying particular emphasis on themselves and their students for the necessity to memorize.[108] The rabbis passed on various rules for strengthening the memory, but stressed above all the principle of continual verbal repetition. Consider the story of R. Johanan b. Zakkai. The story tells of R. Zakkai in the camp of the Roman Vespasian outside the Old City in the 1st century CE. After R. Zakkai had been received in audience by Vespasian for the first time: *"They seized him and locked him up with seven locks, and asked him what time it was at night, and he told them, and what time it was during the day, and he told them. And how did our master Johanan ben Zakkai know? From his recitation of the Mishanah"* (Midrash Echa 1:31). In other words R. Johanan not only knew the entire Mishnah by heart, but he knew just how long it took to recite each paragraph, and how much time he needed to get through it all. This account is a proper reflection of the orality and emphasis on memorization in the rabbinic world of the 1st century CE. There are more examples of the emphasis put on repetition as the key mnemonic tool. R. Sheshet was in the habit of repeating everything he had learned every thirtieth day after which he would lean against a door and say: *"Rejoice, my soul, rejoice, my soul! To you I have read the Scriptures (from memory); for you I have repeated"* (b. Pes. 68b). And of other rabbis it is said that when the Angel of Death stood at their threshold, they bade for a respite, during which time they would repeat from heart all they knew of the Torah (b. Ket 77b).[109] Obviously memorization was the linchpin that held together all of the oral teachings in the rabbinic world. Repetition was the key of keys implemented by the rabbis to impregnate the heart and mind with Torah in the rabbinic period. This period could be considered the golden age of memorization and gives us the most insight into the emphasis placed upon memorization and the techniques used to facilitate memorization in the rabbinic world.

The Professional Memorizer in the Rabbinic Period

Even though the designation *tanna* (lit. repeater), referring to an official memorizer of oral Torah, appears for the first time in connection to R. Akiva in the 1st century CE, the office was solidified later in the rabbinic colleges into something of an institution. These *tannaim* were counted on as being living books, connected with the rabbinic college for the purpose of memorizing and repeating aloud the oral texts in the classroom. They were purely and simply verbatim repeaters at the disposal of the teachers and students of the colleges.

107. Daniel Henry Rops, *Daily Life in Palestine at the time of Christ* pg. 270
108. Birger Gerhardsson, *Memory and Manuscript* pg. 150
109. ibid pg. 169

It was with the aid of such skilled professional memorizers that the rabbis in the colleges preserved the oral Torah in an authorized form until written copies began to be of official importance. Lecturers in the college would ask such *tannaim* to recite a portion of the oral Torah the lecturer intended to expound or to refresh the rabbi's memory of the exact wording of a particular passage. The *tanna* would then with ease say from memory the requested passage (j. Ma'aser Sheni 5:1).

The Talmud warns that despite their ability to recite long passages without error, some professional memorizers were not always to be treated as scholars. The rabbis characterized many of these living books as follows: *"The magician mumbles and does not understand what he says; similarly, the memorizer recited but does not understand"* (b. Sotah 22a). This does not mean that no *tanna* had any insight into the interpretation of the text, but apparently many *tanna* were not at a level of rabbinic education that included the ability to interpret the texts meaning. This phenomenon of knowing the verbatim wording of a text but not knowing its interpretation is something we will see again later during the modern period among the Shass Pollak.

The rabbis were conscious of the variable accuracy and reliability of the different oral traditions. Some *tanna* became famous for their extreme precision, and could become the teacher's living reference book. Yet other *tannaim* were regarded as being less reliable. R. Benjamin b. Jefet was placed beneath R. Hiyya b. Abba, since the latter gave more careful consideration to the texts and repeated them every month before his teacher (b. Ber 38b). The amount of memorized texts by the *tannaim* also varied. Some had only a few collections of texts at their mental disposal, while others had them all. As we shall see later, this phenomenon exists today in the Silberstein yeshiva, where some of the students have half of the Mishnah memorized and others have almost the whole corpus memorized. We have a Talmudic statement defining the standard in Amoraic times of one who would be counted a fully qualified *tanna*. Such a one must: *"repeat (from memory) all the most important collections of tradition: Mishnah, Sifra, Sifre and Tosefta, in the same way as a Scripture specialist must know the whole of Scripture accurately from memory"* (b. Qic 49b).[110]

Not only did the *tannaim* serve as living books but they also were secondary teachers in the college. The *tannaim* knew the Mishnah or the Talmud with their correct cantillations by heart and trained students also to memorize them by rote. Cantillation or reciting a text in a singing manner with clear indication of short and long intervals was of high practical importance in their oral world. The Mishnah and Talmud at that time carried neither punctuation marks nor vowel signs and even when it did one had to be taught the correct recitation. Therefore, both the pronunciation of the individual words and the correct division of a sentence into its various components depended entirely on memorization.[111] Since this teaching is strictly oral, if it was not faithfully handed down over the generations the proper cantillation would be lost. For example, the Yemenite Jews, who to this day retained the ancient institution of the *tannaim* possess a sound knowledge of the correct pronunciation of the Talmudic texts, especially of the Mishnah, a tradition lost to many European Jews.[112] The office of the *tannaim* became less important or even extinct in some parts of the Jewish world beginning sometime in the medieval period when written books became more frequently published and all the labor that would have to go into producing a living book seemed less practical.

---

110. ibid pg. 99
111. William Graham, *Beyond the Written Word* pg. 199
112. ibid pg. 200

Hasidic Storytelling

As we leave the medieval period we still find examples of an emphasis on orality in Jewish thought and practice. In the 18th century, Hasidism vigorously encouraged storytelling, moving it from the periphery to the center of their worship and missionary work. Many rebbes praised storytelling as a mitzvah and a spiritual practice; they reflected on it deeply and taught about its significance. In the world of Judaism there was and is nothing like it outside Hasidism. Not only did rebbes often tell stories, they instructed their Hasidism to do likewise. As a result, telling and listening to tales became as popular as never before and were enthusiastically embraced by masses of ordinary Hasidism. This revival of religious storytelling played a major role in the rapid growth of the Hasidic movement to this day. The place of storytelling in Hasidism goes back to its founder, Israel Baal Shem Tov in 1777. For ten years he wandered about from one place to another in Eastern Europe, to draw people to Judaism by storytelling. He and his fellow rhapsodists told such stories as the books of Moses, the tales of the prophets, and the sages of the Talmud from memory. For religion to reach the common people it must be presented in a popular way, and stories do just that.[113] As I noted in the introduction and as we see here, the broad masses of a population are more open to the appeal of rhetoric than to any written force.

The Professional Memorizer in the Modern Period

Let us move forward to the 20th century and see if memorization still played a key role in Judaism. In 1917 psychologist George Stratton's attention was directed towards a special achievement in Talmudic memorization similar to what we saw in the *tanna* during the rabbinic period. The Babylonian Talmud consists of twelve large folio volumes comprising thousands of pages. All the printed editions of the Talmud have exactly the same number of pages and the same words on each page to foster memorization. Stratton's friend, Rev. Philipson, interviewed a Jewish man who knew like many of the *tannaim* of old the whole Talmud by heart. Philipson would open one of the volumes of the Talmud, say the tractate *Berakhot*, at page ten; place a pin on a word, say the fourth word in line eight; then would ask the man what word is in this same spot on page ten or any other page; the pin would be pressed through the volume until it reached page ten, and the man's memory would say the word and it was found to be correct. The man had visualized or mentally photocopied the whole Talmud on his brain. Many people would say this is impossible, but the Talmud was written and is formatted to be memorized and with proper dedication can be entirely memorized.

The technical name which was used by the Jews to designate these memory experts was *Shass Pollak*. *Shass* is the abbreviation for the Hebrew terms for the Talmud, and *Pollak* is Pole; nearly all these memory experts came from Poland; a *Shass Pollak* then is a Pole who has memorized the entire contents of the Talmud and is able to give exhibitions of his mnemonic powers. Philipson witnessed, though, that the achievement was purely mechanical like the earlier criticism we heard of some *tanna* in the rabbinic period: *"The magician mumbles and does not understand what he says; similarly, the memorizer recited but does not understand"* (b. Sotah 22a). The Pole could not interpret the Talmud though he knew its entire contents by heart.[114] The mnemonic ability of these men did not represent the normal emphasis put on memorization

---

113. Yitzhak Buxbaum, *Storytelling and Spirituality in Judaism* pg. 7
114. Ulric Neisser, *Memory Observed* pg. 312

in the world of Judaism at that time. And we don't know from the interviews why these men memorized the whole Talmud, nor if they functioned like the ancient *tannaim* in their colleges in Poland. It is very likely that what we will observe in regards to the normative importance placed upon memorization today in Judaism was the same as it was last century.

The Rabbi in the Modern Period

In order to get an idea of what level of importance is laid on memorization of the oral and written Torah within Judaism today I interviewed R. Shlomo, at the Return yeshiva on Mt. Zion. Like the rabbis of old who emphasized repetition as the key to memorization, R. Shlomo said: *"the Torah world is a world of repetition. A person who does not repeat is like a person who sows and does not reap. We were always told as kids that we must repeat the commandments again and again. There were no other techniques we used to memorize other than verbal repetition. The only way we memorize is by repeating. We were told repeating it 100 times is not like repeating it 101 times."* R. Shlomo came from an orthodox background so I asked him if he could tell me what emphasis was laid on memorization in his formative educational years: *"The yeshiva I went to as a kid did not ask us to memorize Bible texts by heart but there are schools like that such as the Zilberman yeshiva in the Old City. There was in my later education an emphasis not on memorizing Bible verses but rabbinic cases and opinions."* I asked R. Shlomo to tell me about oral tradition and transmission: *"I follow an oral tradition that was originally given at Mt. Sinai by HaShem to Moses. These include such things as meat and milk and how are you to live with your wife. Growing up we didn't even have to try and memorize all these commandments; they just become second nature because we grew up in an oral world. It is a world of habitual memorization. Your parents teach you to memorize by doing an action again and again and you thereby memorize it by not even knowing it. The goal is not to just memorize this and that but to memorize it and carry out the action with the right motive."*

I asked him about the emphasis on memorizing *halacha* and the Bible in the Jewish world. He said: *"In my education we memorized much more Gomorra and Mishnah than Bible in order to try and learn things that apply to daily life. We memorize sayings that have to do with everything from daily life such as a prayer when I tie my shoes and eat an apple."* I then asked Shlomo if he knew of anyone like the Shass Pollack who had the entire Talmud memorized: *"When I was a kid I knew of a man named R. Yoshua Cohen who had the whole Talmud memorized. We used to read to him from a page and he could tell you what page it was on through the whole Talmud. Not only did R. Yoshua have a lot memorized, but many hazzan today who weekly read from Moses in the synagogue know the first five books by heart because they have been reading them for so many years. Even though they know Moses by heart, in the synagogue service they must read from the text."* Finally I asked him how popular memorization was today. He said *"It is very rare to find Jews today who know many of the writings word by word from heart."*

After I talked with R. Shlomo I came away with the impression that whether he knew it or not he was talking to me in memorized oral Torah language. He quoted or paraphrased numerous portions from the Talmud. I think he represents your average Jewish student/rabbi's view of memorization in the 21st century. That *"it is very rare to find Jews today who know many of the writings word by word from heart,"* but on the other hand know portions of the *halachaic* writings from heart not because they deliberately went out to memorize them but because they live and move in an oral world and were memorized as part of their childhood education and stayed in their long-term memory because of constant verbal repetition.

Conclusion

We must stand afar from our western cultural mindset of solely written transmission and move across to a middle-eastern oral mindset to better understand the emphasis and favor put on memorization over the ages. As we have read, memorization was and is a highly sought after endowment in the world of Judaism. The ability and drive to memorize complete books seems to have been limited to those whose profession revolved around the Torah. Just how much your average Jewish person had memorized during the times we traced is impossible to tell. And the testimonies of living persons today seems to point towards vast memorization of the Torah to be for the very few. I would like to finish this section with a story. Charles Glass, a journalist in Syria described time spent in a village there 20 years ago. In the remote places of Syria he visited an archaeologist studying the similarities between ancient and modern villages. The archaeologist told Glass: *"There are so many similarities that it is as if the village we're in now, if you came back in 2000 years, would be the same as the village we're digging up at the moment...Of course, there are implements they didn't have like the oil drums, the gas stoves or whatever. But everything else is the same. The mud houses are the same and the wooden ceilings were made in the same way. The design of the town is the same now as it was then. If you just look around the village, you don't have to look far to see the same thing in the ruins. You can see yourself how Biblical it is."*[115] As well, if you just look around Jerusalem you don't have to look far to see those who like the living books of old, have memorized vast amounts of oral and written Torah. Sure, the time and technologies have changed but these living books still walk Jerusalem's streets. You can see how rabbinic their world still is. Yet just as the remote village of today has not changed much over the millennia I suspect peoples' attitudes toward memorizing have pretty much stayed the same as well. It was and is the rare exception to find memorization experts in the world of Judaism but the common people did and still have a meager amount of prayers and portions of the oral and written Torah memorized.

---

115. *Expository Times vol. 106* pg. 363

CHAPTER V

Who Memorized in Christianity?

In this chapter we want to point out different individuals and institutions that memorized the Bible and liturgy from the time of Jesus, the early Church, through the Byzantine and medieval periods up until today in the Middle Eastern Church. In doing so I hope to highlight the level of necessity put on memorization by that niche of the populace at different periods of time and consider why they went to such great efforts to memorize.

Memorization: Jesus and His Audience

We know that Jesus was often addressed by his followers as Teacher, but did he make his style of preaching deliberately memorizable? The poetical structure wherein Jesus crafted his words helped preserve them intact for future transmission. Even the sayings of Jesus included an imperative to remember them. The Gospels say that Jesus taught his listeners much in the form of concise parables. In other words Jesus was a *moshel,* a Jewish master of wisdom. The sayings of Jesus can be divided into aphoristic and narrative parables. 65% of this total number is not more than two verses long. The aphoristic ones consist of brief words, one or two sentences long. The narrative ones are parables, 60% of which are not more than four verses long. Just as the rabbis taught that *"a sharp peppercorn is better than a basket of gourds"* (b. Meg. 7a), the most characteristic feature of Jesus' sayings is their brevity to aid memorization.[116]

Teachers like Jesus, who presented a similar message to different audiences at different places, developed a basic message which encapsulated their main views in a way that proved effective in order for the speaker and the audience to remember them. For example, the occurrence of two versions of Jesus' teaching, one set on a hill and one on a plain, is not surprising. Jesus was engaged in teaching in an oral world, and he frequently repeated himself. If a speech was repeatedly delivered in slightly different versions in the presence of the disciples, given their devotion to Jesus and the memorable nature of what he said, the audience would in good Jewish fashion have had no difficulty in memorizing and repeating what he said at some later time.[117] Repetition was the most often used mnemonic tool in this oral milieu. The sayings of Jesus were then memorized, repeated, applied and past on at first by oral transmission. Among the early Christians who thought of Jesus as among other things a rabbi (Mk 9:5, 10:51, 11:21), would favor such a way of preserving his teaching by rote memorization. In such circles it would be entirely natural to treat the sayings of Jesus in just this way. The book of Acts also speaks of *"remembering the words of the Lord Jesus,"* (Acts 20:35) and quotes words of Jesus that never made there way into the written Gospel transmission.[118]

---

116. Birger Gerhardsson, *The Secret of the Transmission of the Unwritten Jesus Tradition* pg. 10
117. George Kennedy, *New Testament Interpretation through Rhetorical Criticism* pg. 68
118. Edgar J. Goodspeed *An Introduction to the New Testament* pg. 126

The organization of the new Jewish Christian community inside Israel was accomplished by the continuation of inherited Jewish teachings and by the recourse to sayings of Jesus that were transmitted at first in the oral tradition as we earlier read from the Church Fathers. These materials were passed down in order to serve as instructional materials for the early church. There was no need for the production of authoritative written documents within a Jewish context. Founding apostles used personal visits in order to nurture the new communities. Written letters were needed only when their personal presence was made impossible.

Memorization and Paul

The letters of Paul give us glimpses of the form in which the memorized oral sayings of Jesus were circulated. That form was an oral form and evidently learned by many Christians when they entered the Church. This is why Paul can say: *"I myself received from the Lord the account that I passed on to you"* (1 Cor. 11:23). The words "received, passed on" reflect the practice of oral tradition, the handing down by memorization from one person to another. This was congenial to the Jewish mindset. It was a point of pride in Judaism and even in the early Church not to commit to writing their oral traditions but to preserve them from memory unaltered as we earlier saw from the testimonies of the Church Fathers.

In the letters that Paul wrote there are many instances when he quotes sayings of Jesus he must have leaned from memory. In Romans 12:14, we find the sentence, *"Bless those who persecute you; bless and do not curse them"*, and in 1 Cor. 4:12-13, *"When reviled, we bless; when persecuted, we endure."* This phrase may be compared with the one we find in Luke 6:27-28: *"Love your enemies, do good to those who hate you, bless those who curse you, pray for those who abuse you."* The meaning and wording resemble a remarkable similarity. In Romans 13:7 we read: *"Pay to all what is due them, taxes to whom taxes are due, revenue to whom revenue is due."* This reminds us of Mark 12:17: *"Give to Caesar the things that are Caesar's and to God the things that are God's."* Again the wording and the point are the same. Another example is found in Romans 14:14: *"I know and am persuaded in the Lord Jesus that nothing is unclean in itself; but it is unclean for anyone who thinks it unclean."* This resembles Mark 7:15: *"There is nothing outside a person that by going in can defile, but the things that come out are what defile."* The sayings of Jesus play a key role in Paul's writings, especially with regard to the order of the life of the new Christian community. This makes perfect sense seeing that Jesus is the Lord of Paul. There are six explicit references to sayings which Paul quotes from Jesus (1 Cor. 7:10, 25; 9:14; 11:23-26; 1 Thess. 4:15-17). In addition to these there are at least ten sayings which Paul quotes that allude to sayings of Jesus (Rom. 12:14, 17, 18; 13:7; 14:10, 13, 14; 1 Thess. 5:2, 13). Paul had memorized the sayings of Jesus which were orally transmitted in the early Church. Just whom Paul heard these orally transmitted sayings from, the Bible nor any Church authority informs us.

It is a fair conjecture that the process of reducing evangelical tradition to writing appeared soon after Christianity began to spread in the Gentile world. The Jew was so adept in the use of oral transmission that he had little need of transmission by the written page. Jews did not write Torah, they depended on memorization but not so with the Greek. Writing was the fixed custom of the 1st century Graeco-Roman world. As soon as Paul and the first Christian missionaries began to teach their Gentile converts a demand likely arose for Christian written literature.[119]

Memorization and the Early Church

Let us fast forward into the next few centuries and see who memorized in the early church and what level of significance was given to memorization? Irenaeus from the 2nd century relates what he carried in his memory as that which he had received in teachings from Polycarp: *"I can even name the place where the blessed Polycarp sat and taught and where he went out and in. I remember his way of life, what he looked like, the addresses he delivered to the people, how he told of his time with John and with the others who had seen the Lord, how he remembered their words and what he had heard from them about the Lord, about his miracles, and about his teaching. As one who had received this from eyewitnesses of the Word of Life, Polycarp retold everything in accordance with the Scriptures. I listened to this then, because of the grace of God which was given me, carefully, copying it down not on paper, but on my heart. And I repeat it constantly in genuine form by the grace of God."* [120] We may note that early Christian oral tradition like Judaism is linked with an authoritative spokesman. This is an extremely characteristic factor in an environment in which tradition and authority play an important part. Who it is that communicates a tradition is of vital importance, as is the question: from whom did he derive it? When Irenaeus quotes a tradition, he often gives a chain of reliable sources: he heard it from the elders who in their turn had been disciples of the Apostles.[121] Secondly, we see that Irenaeus claims to have learned the tradition from memory. We can see the great value placed upon faithful and exact memorization.

Papias also in the 2nd century expressed his reverence for those who speak of *"the commandments which are given by the Lord for faith, and which derive from the very truth."*[122] This concept common among the Church Fathers is a close parallel to rabbinic tradition. Papias said: *"And then whenever someone came who as a disciple had accompanied the elders I used to search for the words of the elders: what Andrew or what Peter had said or what Philip or what Thomas or what James or what John or what Matthew or any other disciple of the Lord, or what Aristion or what John the Elder, the disciples of the Lord, say."*[123] Here we may observe a method of oral transmission of the same type used in rabbinic Judaism: Rabbi X. said in Rabbi Y's name. This is the witness of an early Church authority, who says in the next sentence that he relied less upon the written word than upon that which came from the living human voice. Papias had not copied down the traditions concerning Jesus in writing but had learned them carefully from memory. The fact that he later wrote five books is another matter.[124]

Memorization and Byzantine Fathers

As we enter the Byzantine Period we see the continuation on the emphasis of memorization by the early

---

119. H.E. Dana, *The Ephesian Tradition* pg. 12
120. Eusebius, *Hist. Eccl. V.20*
121, Birger Gerhardsson, *Memory and Manuscript* pg. 204
122. Eusebius, *Hist. Eccl. III.39*
123. Irenaeus, *Adv. Haer. III 5.1*
124. Eusebius, *Hist. Eccl. III.39*

Church. As we earlier read that many in the Church today memorize by the often hearing of the spoken word in the services, so St. Anthony in the 3rd century learned the whole Bible by heart merely from hearing it read aloud. The fact that he never saw a copy of the written word is what astonished his contemporaries.[125] Memorization was vital to keeping the mind spiritually on track and avoiding mental fornication. John Cassian in the 4th century, who we earlier read was influenced on the need for memorization by his exposure to the Pachomion Rule described the struggle as follows: *"Our minds think of some passage of a Psalm (from memory). But it is taken away from us without our noticing it, and the spirit slips on to some other text of Scripture. It begins to think about it, but before it has been fully considered, another text slides into the memory and drives out the previous one. Meanwhile another one arrives and our mind turns to another meditation. So the spirit rolls along from Psalm to Psalm, leaps from the gospel to Paul, from Paul to the prophets, from there it is carried off to holy stories. Ever on the move, forever wandering, it is tossed along through all the body of Scripture, unable to settle on anything. If I am praying my mind thinks about a Psalm or another reading. If I am singing it is preoccupied with something other than what is in the Psalm I am chanting. Three things keep a wandering mind in place: vigils, meditation, and prayer."*[126] As John wrote, the mind never stops thinking and the only way to preserve the mind was with the washing of the water of the memorized Word of God.

Augustine remarked in the 4th century that even if you have the whole Bible word for word memorized, you still need to recall it in summary when you come to teach beginners: *"But, even if we have memorized the words verbatim, we should not just recite by rote the whole Pentateuch, and the entire book of Judges, Kings, and the whole of the Gospels and Acts…but when teaching select certain things as being more worthy to be examined closely…dwell on it a piece at a time and offer it for inspection and wonder by the minds of the audience."*[127] Augustine's remarks make it plausible that many of those who were teachers of the Bible during this time could have almost the whole Bible memorized verbatim. Augustine also commented on the importance of memorization in preparation for the sermon: *"Before I come before you, I mentally compose in advance what I will say to you. When I have composed what I will say to you, then the word is in my memory."*[128]

In the 4th century, Jerome who was also under the influence of Pachomion Rule comments on Ezekiel 3:5: *"Eating the book is the starting-point of reading and of basic history. When by diligent meditation we store away the book of the Lord in our memorial treasury, our belly is filled spiritually and our guts are satisfied."* Jerome then links this action of eating the book to memorizing it. Jerome admonishes the reader to store the honey of Scripture in one's own memory.[129] As we have seen in this section many of the men who came out of the Pachomion Rule with its emphasis on memorization themselves were later proponents for memorization in the Church. They considered themselves the links in the chain of memorizing Scripture which connected the early Church to and through the Byzantine period.

---

125. Mary Carruthers, *The Book of Memory* pg. 12
126. Mary Carruthers, *The Craft of Thought* pg. 83
127. Mary Carruthers, *The Book of Memory* pg. 159
128. ibid pg. 207
129. ibid pg. 44

Memorization and the Byzantine Monk

What level of importance was laid on memorization of the Bible in the Byzantine monastery? The command to remember is characteristic of the Bible, memorably throughout the one book that most monks learned by heart, the Psalms. As mentioned earlier, the Psalms were the foundation of memorization; as a novice one learned many of them and could recite them straight through. If there was one verse to be written on the heart of the monk it was: *"Come to my help, O God; Lord, hurry to my rescue"* (Psalm 69:1). This verse ensured that in any daily activity or temptation, the monk would be in a state of constant recitation and prayer. An excerpt from an anonymous monk's prayer will give an example of the emphasis put on recalling this verse from memory in a time of need: "I am assailed by a desire for good eating. I seek out food of which a hermit should know nothing. Into my filthy solitude come the fragrances of royal dishes and I feel myself dragged unwillingly along by my longing for them. And so I must say, *"Come to my help, O God; Lord, hurry to my rescue." The due hour has come to bid me eat, but bread disgusts me and I am held back from my natural necessity. And so I must howl aloud, "Come to my help, O God; Lord, hurry to my rescue." …When I have not been able to save myself by my many groans and cries, I must cry out, "Come to my help, O God; Lord, hurry to my rescue."*[130] The memorized Scriptures were the first line of defense to be immediately called upon from the heart during times of trial. Let us continue to observe the emphasis put on memorization within the walls of the monastery. When Cyriacus served as precentor at the monastery of Theodosius in the 3rd century, he would not cease knocking on the wooden beam to awake the monks for prayer until he had finished reciting to himself all of Psalm 119 from memory.[131] In the Pachomian Ruled monasteries, monks assembled each evening after their meal, at which time it was practice for *"each one to pronounce what he knew of the Holy Scriptures…when they were seated, each one brought forth the saying he had learned or that he head heard from the lips of another."*[132] Repeated allusions in the sources to learning and reciting the Scriptures by heart reflect how fundamental a feature of memorization was. Indeed, in characterizing the Tabennesiot monks, Palladius notes that, along with the various kinds of manual labor required of them: *"they all learned the Scriptures by heart."* It was just not within the walls of the monastery where memory was emphasized but in the written book. In the 4th century pseudo-*Clementine Recognitiones,* the author causes Peter to speak of the power of memorization. He had adopted the habit of forcing himself to awaken after midnight: *"I have adopted the habit of recalling in my memory the words of my Lord which I heard from himself, and because of my longing for them I force my mind and my thoughts to be roused, so that, awakening to them, and recalling and repeating each one of them, I keep them in my memory."*[133] A 6th century text, *Regula Magistri,* advises that monks on a journey who had not yet memorized the Psalms should provide themselves with tables on which the text was written, so that when they stopped they could sharpen their memory with the help of a companion.[134] Memorization, especially of the Psalter was the fundamental spiritual discipline during the Byzantine period.

---

130. Mary Carruthers, *The Craft of Thought* pg. 76
131. Joseph Patrich *Sabas, Leader of Palestinian Monasticism* pg. 233
132. William Graham, *Beyond the Written Word* pg. 131
133. Mary Carruthers, *The Craft of Thought* pg. 77
134. Mary Carruthers, *The Book of Memory* pg. 88

Memorization and Women

There is unfortunately not much written on women and memorization in the early Church sources. A source we do have shows that it was not only men who memorized. Macrina the sister of Gregory of Nyssa established a monastery at Annisa in the 4th century. Gregory wrote of his sister: *"She was especially well versed in (memorizing) the Psalms, going through each part of the Psalter at the proper time: when she got up or did her daily tasks or rested, when she sat down to eat or rose from the table, when she went to bed or rose from it for prayer, she had the Psalter with her at all times, like a good and faithful traveling companion."*[135] We can thereby assume as head of the monastery, Macrina also encouraged the memorization and daily recitation of the Psalms to the women who abode at her monastery.

Memorization in the Medieval Period

As we make our way into the medieval period we continue to find an emphasis on orality and memorization even though they often lived in a printed world. The 6th century Rule of Ferreolus observed: *"anyone who wishes to be worthy of the name of monk is forbidden to be ignorant of letters; he must also hold all of the Psalms in his memory."* In the 9th century Vision of Wetti a monastic dream poem, Wetti is in spiritual torment and gives full attention to chanting the Psalms from memory. An angel arrives and urges him to continue doing this, and even gives him another assignment, to repeat Psalm 119 over and over. Bruno of Querfort from the 10th century wrote: *"Be seated within your cell as though in paradise; cast to the rear of your memory everything distracting, becoming alert and focused on your thoughts as a good fisherman on the fish. One pathway to this state is through reciting the Psalms; do not neglect to do this. If you cannot manage to get through them all at one sitting as you used to do with the fervor of a novice, take pains to chant the psalms in your spirit."*[136] The spiritual emphasis placed on the memorization of the Psalter is still of fundamental value hundreds of years later from the time we first read about it at the Pachomian community.

According to medieval Christians memorizing provided textual weapons to defend the mind against the enemy. Peter of Celle from the 12th century wrote: *"One who does not devote himself to holy reading disarms his ramparts of a1000 shields which might hang down from them. How quickly and easily is the little citadel of your cell captured if you do not now defend yourself with God's help and the shield of the sacred page? Take projectiles from your bookcases so that when you are struck you may strike back at the one who struck you."*[137] Much of Peter's advice is couched in the language of meditative reading, which included the language of an educated memory. These images of the "little citadel of your cell," of the "bookcases" in which are stored the weapons which with to defend yourself have a mnemonic technique. Peter's audience likely did not have bookcases in their cells, for the monastery book chests were in the cloister, and these monks did not have private cells. So the "bookcase" in "your cell" should be understood figuratively, as the monk's memory, in which the Bible verses he has armed himself with by heart are kept ready at hand. The bedroom of the mind is what medieval anchorites called cubiculum. Its goal is cognitive creation, and its matrix is the secret places of one's own mind, the matters secreted away in the inventory of memory, stored

135. Joseph Patrich *Sabas, Leader of Palestinian Monasticism* pg. 487
136. Mary Carruthers, *The Craft of Thought* pg. 112
137. ibid pg. 108

and recalled, collated and gathered up by the craft of mnemonics. Withdrawal to one's chamber indicates a state of mind, the entry to the place of meditative silence. Moral character was developed by means of responses inculcated by the ruminative reflection upon memorized texts. The texts were committed by memorizing exercises, notably repetition, which primarily consisted of saying over and over to one self, either quietly or loudly, what the person wished to engrave on their memory. After the last reading of the night general silence is usually observed until the Night Office. The time alone in the room is about the practice of meditation, and night time was considered in classical pedagogy the best time for memory work.[138] Hugo de Folieto also in the 12th century wrote on the concept of memorizing: *"Therefore we devour and digest the book, when we read the words of God. Many indeed read, but from their reading they remain ignorant…but others devour and digest the holy books and are not ignorant because their memory does not let go of the rules for life whose meaning it can grasp."*[139] From de Folieto's comments there were certain intensities of individuals in regards to memorization. Some monks were known for having a stronger passion on the necessity to memorize the Bible and others seem not to have been very zealous for hiding God's word in their heart.

The 13th century scholar Thomas Aquinas was known for his memorization skills. It is written: *"his memory was extremely rich and retentive. Whatever he had once read and grasped he never forgot."*[140] His works *Summa Theologial* and *Catena Aurea* were dictated to his scribe from memory. Proper preparation of material, rigid order, and complete concentration were the requirements Thomas defined in his discourses on memory.[141] Richard de Bury in the 14th century commented on how he depended on the industry of others to collect memorized books to pass on by oral transmission: *"First of all it behooves you to eat (memorize) the book with Ezekiel, that the belly of your memory may be sweetened within…What an infinite power of (living) books lies down in Paris or Athens, and yet sounds at the same time in Britain and Rome. In truth while they lie quietly they are moved, while holding their own places they are born everywhere in the minds of the listeners."*[142] Peter of Ravenna in the 15th century wrote a work on the art of memory, stating that a well-trained memory is most like a book: *"For I daily read all my lectures of Canon Law without a book; but if I should have a book before my eyes, I deliver the textual concordances and glosses from memory so that I should not seem to omit the least syllable."*[143] Though many of these men lived in a printed world, they respected and also adapted parts of the oral world into their daily life. Memorization of the Bible, was a fundamental spiritual activity that continued its way to and through the medieval period Church.

Memorization in the Modern Period

Following the advice of the early Church Fathers that what can be learned from a frozen book cannot be compared to what can be learned from a living person I went on a quest to personally inquire of members of the Middle Eastern Church in Jerusalem what their position on memorization was today. We must let the

---

138. ibid pg. 174
139. ibid pg. 167
140. ibid pg. 3
141. ibid pg. 8
142. ibid pg. 90
143. ibid pg. 109

men speak for themselves and see if we can discern what level of importance is laid on memorization of the Bible and liturgy within the different denominations of the Church in the Middle East.

Copts

In order to get an idea of what level of importance is laid on memorization of the Bible and liturgy within the Coptic Church I interviewed Father Dumadius at the Church of the Holy Sepluchre. He said: *"We keep much of the holy liturgy in our hearts. For example we have in our mind the whole liturgy of the Holy Songs of Midnight. We do not necessarily follow along in the text during the readings in our daily services but speak the liturgy from memory. We don't know the entire holy liturgy that we use on special holidays but know much of it by heart. It is because we speak and hear the daily liturgy for such a long period of time that we have them memorized. Not all of us know the entire Holy Bible from memory but we do know significant portions of it from memory such as the Psalms. Yet some priest and monks do know the entire Holy Bible from heart. All you have to do is speak one word from a verse to them and they can continue to tell the verse(s) from memory. Some priests and monks pray the same 75 Psalms from memory daily. Some pray all 150 Psalms daily but need to use a book because they don't have all of them memorized. In the Coptic monastery there is a tremendous emphasis on memorization of the liturgy and the Psalms to this day."*

Armenians

In order to get an idea of what level of importance is laid on memorization of the Bible and liturgy within the Armenian Church I interviewed Father Gomidass Sherbetdjianan, an Armenian priest in the Church of the Holy Sepluchre. He said: *"From my experience there is no need to memorize today because we have the accessibility of books. Memorizing is not the solution to any spiritual problem nor is it an important aspect in the church today. The most important thing is that we have to understand and practice the Bible. To the best of my knowledge, there were not certain periods in Armenian Church history where memorization was considered more important than in other times. There were exceptions, but there never was an emphasis that the Bible needed to be memorized in any sphere, not even in seminary. I personally don't know of anyone in the history of the Armenian Church that has been singled out as being extraordinarily skilled in memorization. We don't set out with the objective to memorize. Slowly by slowly we accumulate the memorization of certain texts by hearing and reading them over and over in the services."*

Syrians

In order to get an idea of what level of importance is laid on memorization of the Bible and liturgy within the Syrian Church I interviewed Abu Shimon at the Church of St. Mark in the Old City. He said: *"We do have a tradition to keep many of the Biblical and liturgical texts in our hearts, especially from the Psalter. We find that during times of temptation the memorized Word is very important. The process of memorizing texts is deliberate; it is acquired from daily services, personal devotions, and seminary training. Before ordination to become a monk or parish priest, or to be involved in any priesthood services, the candidate has to learn special prayers by heart to prepare him for service. Of the prayers or texts we use weekly, on simple days, I know 90% of them by heart and know of people who know many but not all of St. Ephrem's writings from heart. Even though we have certain Bible verses memorized, we do not speak the Bible from memory in our services. It is our custom to read the Bible exactly as it is written so that one word is not missed. As a general rule we don't stress memorization but rely on reading the written word in all spheres. When we read and pray by heart in our personal devotions we feel that our mind is more easily apt to wander when we don't use a book. We do think it is important to memorize, but we insist on looking at the text when reading and praying.*

There are circumstances that do not permit us to have a book, so then we must rely on whatever we have previously memorized to fulfill our task. For example, if I am called upon to pray for a sick person and do not have a prayer book with me it is important to know the prayers by heart in order to be able to pray for that person."

Ethiopians

In order to get an idea of what level of importance is laid on memorization of the Bible and liturgy within the Ethiopian Church I interviewed various members at the Church of the Holy Sepluchre. The interviews with the monks were often difficult because of their lack of English and my lack of Arabic but through our conversations, observing their services and rituals I have a good idea of how important memorization is to them. From their testimonies I observed that all of the monks were taught to memorize the Psalms and their liturgy via oral transmission from the grade school up. Since the language of the service is in Ge'ez it is almost impossible for many of the lay people to understand what is being said since the lingua franca of Ethiopia is Amharic. This is analogues to Latin being spoken in the Catholic services in the USA before the 1960's. From my interviews I found that the vast majority of the monks spend hours a day repeating aloud their memorized texts. They often do this in groups of two with the elder monk correcting the pronunciation of the younger monk when he is reading from Dawid. The monks always read the text when they are reviewing even though they likely have most of it memorized. I was told that there are some priests that don't understand the interpretation of a large amount of the Ge'ez language but still consider the text inspired and find it religiously edifying to memorize and repeat such portions. I was also told that the services are almost entirely oral and it is not unusual to observe the priests telling the portions of the Bible and liturgy from memory in Ge'ez to the lay people.

Greek Orthodox

In order to get an idea of what level of importance is laid on memorization of the Bible and liturgy within the Greek Orthodox Church I interviewed the Greek Orthodox Patriarch of Jerusalem in the Old City. I asked his Beatitude if he could help inform me on the subject matter within the Church but he decided to take the interview in a different direction which was fine with me.

His main emphasis was that memorizing to a high capacity is a gift from the Father and to take heed lest you then become puffed up. He suggested that I memorize portions of Job and challenge myself with the notion of struggle, dying daily and looking to the cross. He said we need prototypes and examples today of Christians who memorize and orally proclaim the written word and was enthused to listen to me tell him part of the Apocalypse. When he was a child he first memorized the Creed of Faith, basic prayers and numerous

Bible verses. He quoted something from the Gospels for me during discussion. He encouraged me to keep in mind the parable of the talents and to turn my talent into something numerous times fold and stressed the importance of speaking the Word from memory to audiences. His Beatitude was exceedingly encouraging and sent me away with gifts.

In order to get another idea of what level of importance was and is laid on memorization of the Bible and liturgy within the Greek Orthodox Church I interviewed Father Ioannes, a Greek Orthodox monk at the Monastery of Temptation in Jericho. He said: *"In my experience there is not an importance laid on memorization at any level in the Greek Orthodox Church from the seminary to the monastery. Yet if a particular individual feels led to memorize so be it, but we still are commanded to read from the Bible and prayer books in our services to avoid any error. Nobody tells the liturgy from memory in the service even though they likely know it all by heart, they still read it. When I read in my cell, I do not read aloud or move my lips but always read silently from a text. I don't know of anyone in the past or today who was known for memorizing an exceptional amount of our sacred writings."*

Latins

In order to get an idea of what level of importance is laid on memorization of the Bible and liturgy within the Catholic Church I interviewed Father Matthew, a Catholic Priest at the Ecole Biblique in Jerusalem. He said: *"In the Catholic Church there is not much direct emphasis on memorization. There is a bit with young people in Catechism class to get them to memorize basic prayers and doctrines. Most of our memorization would occur naturally during our participation in the mass by hearing and reading aloud the liturgy so many times. There is very little direct emphasis on memorization especially on Scripture. I think there is a modern dislike for memorization. Before 1965 there was great emphasis on memorization of the Catechism. With the change in religious education since then memorization of Scripture and liturgy has passed by the wayside. We have never had the emphasis on memorizing the Bible as some evangelicals have had."*

In order to get another opinion of what level of importance is laid upon memorization in the Latin rite I interviewed Father Gregory at the Church of the Holy Sepluchre. I asked him about the emphasis placed upon memorization in the Latin Church, he said: *"I have never had any priest ask me to memorize any portions of the Bible or liturgy nor have I ever seen a priest speak the Bible or liturgy from memory in the service, they always read from an authoritative text. There is not a need for us to memorize today because we have the accessibility of books. We do not speak the Bible or the liturgy from memory in the services but always read them from the text."* Knowing what others in the East have testified concerning memorizing by hearing the Bible and the liturgy spoken so often I posed the same question to him: *"There are certain portions of the Bible and liturgies that I have memorized because of my daily exposure to them in our services, but we do not go out with the intent in the service or in our personal devotions to memorize the Bible."*

In order to get yet another opinion of what level of importance was and is laid on memorization of the Bible and liturgy within the Catholic Church I interviewed Father Thomas Maier, a White Father at the church of St. Anne's in Jerusalem. He said: *"Because our ministry demands learning a foreign language we spend most of our energy on memorizing foreign languages to minister properly to people in their own tongue. Many of us know the different liturgical texts from memory in different languages to celebrate the*

Eucharist. I for one know it in four different languages.

I memorize certain blessings by heart as a pastoral need in case I need to say the prayers in circumstances which I do not have a text. I also memorize a lot of prayers and songs in order to more effectively minister to children because of the convenience. We do encourage the children to occasionally memorize prayers, etc. I do not know of anyone in the church who is known for having an extraordinary ability to memorize vast portions of the Bible or liturgy. But I do know of fathers who have a tremendous capacity for speaking numerous languages. I know that memorization of the Bible and liturgy was much more emphasized in the previous generations due to their lack of technological advancements that we have today, but the loss of the need to memorize has made its way into the church. The technology is a blessing but it does take away the necessity to memorize. Also in seminary training in previous generations there was an emphasis on memorization of doctrines, Bible, and liturgy but in my generation there is not. We would have to know general doctrines, concepts and contents but not verbatim.

Liturgically speaking we always read the Bible and prayers from a text in the services as an act of humility. Even though I know the prayers by heart I read them to show that I am linked to a written text, to a tradition which I follow. I also read in order to show that I am speaking not my own thoughts but the traditions of the church. I think in community liturgical prayer you can speak texts by heart but there is a danger to turn it into a performance of the priest and the audience would be tempted to say 'oh he is good' when they should think 'oh the text is good.' We must submit ourselves to the written text.

In fact we were always advised that when we are in front of the congregation we must read the written text even though we likely know it by heart out of respect for the congregation. In order to help me memorize a new language I often learn prayers in that language by reading it many times, and then at a point I automatically have it memorized. I don't strive with the intent to memorize the Bible or prayers it naturally comes by reason of often repetition."

Conclusion

In this section we have considered what individuals and institutions have dedicated themselves to memorizing the Bible and the religious benefit which is produced from such labor. Like in Judaism, the Church has almost always moved and lived in an orally dominant world out of choice. The memorization of Scripture was traced from those who heard Jesus, we saw Paul's knowledge of the memorized sayings of Jesus and the great importance put on memorization by the Church Fathers. We observed that memorizing Scripture was a requirement for all novices entering the monastery, as well as women. We also read numerous quotes from the medieval Church which greatly esteemed the orality and memorization of the Bible though they lived in an oral world. It is only until we arrive at the modern period that we see a tremendous decline in the desire to memorize the Bible on an individual basis. This phenomenon is no doubt due to the blessing of a plentiful availability of the written Word of God but at the same time the easy access that we have in the 21st century Church to the Bible through the printed book and technology make it less attractive and required to memorize the Bible knowing all of the time, energy, and effort that goes into such a discipline. Yet the power is in the Word, if we have it just in our hands our enemies might take it from us, if it is just in our heads we will forget it, but if it is written on the tablet of our heart then we possess it, it is ours and as our image will be conformed more to the image of Christ by meditating on it day and night it will be stored up in a safe place which no man can steal from us.

Chapter VI

Memorization at the School and Synagogue

In this chapter we want to explore what level of importance was laid on memorization of the Torah in the home school of the biblical period and the importance of memorization of the oral and written Torah in the school from the rabbinic period and the modern period. We also want to explore the same question in regards to the role memorization played in the synagogue in the rabbinic and modern periods.

The Student in the Biblical Period

What importance was given to memorizing and reciting the Bible in the school of the biblical period? The following verses from Deuteronomy encapsulate the ideal curriculum for education in an early Israelite home: *"Recite them for your children, say them when you are at home and when you are on the way, when you lay down and when you get up,"* (Dt. 6:7) and *"teach them to your children, reciting them when you stay at home"* (Dt. 11:19).

Basic to keeping and obeying the words of the Torah in ancient Israel was memorization, repetition and remembering. Unfortunately many modern translations usually render the phrase in Deuteronomy chapters 6 and 11 *"speak about them"* when a better translation is to "recite" or "perform" the texts orally. Anyone can speak about the Torah but the Torah emphasizes the necessity to memorize and recite it. The Hebrew version emphasizes the aspect of oral presentation, to present or quote the text to your audience. In this case it is the parent to the child. Performing the oral text to the student is the Jewish mode in which instruction happens. This is completely different from modern translations and education, since they turn the process of instruction into an intellectual or interpretive procedure: speak about them, i.e., speak about the verses' content, talk about the underlying meaning of the words not the actual words themselves,[144] when the power is in the actual divine words. The words of the Torah are to be orally performed as the basis of all education by the parent or the teacher to the student during all arenas of daily life.[145]

Let us consider another portion of the Bible and its understanding of the relationship between education and memorization. Many instructions in Proverbs focus on a process that has prominent oral and memorization characteristics like we earlier saw in the New Kingdom Egyptian texts: inclining the ear, hearing the words, applying the heart to the sayings, are just a few. The student of Proverbs is to memorize the teacher's exact words, to *"keep them within your belly"* and then perform them orally, *"establish the words on your lips."* The tablet of the student's heart was the key focus in the teaching texts of Proverbs. A hearing heart or an open ear was the oral medium by which the heart received, memorized and obeyed Torah. The Bible speaks often of having texts *"written on the table of the heart."* The writing metaphor is used to picture a process that is also oral, all of which is focused on the sort of word-for-word verbatim internalization of the Bible

---

144. Eep Talstra, *Texts for Recitation* pg. 68
145. ibid pg. 69

with the goal of the Bible never to leave the lips of the student so they can be recited and obeyed day and night. Let us continue to explore if the same emphasis put on memorizing in biblical Israel transcended to the rabbinic period.

The Student in the Rabbinic Period

In the rabbinic period there was obviously a copy of the written Torah available in certain circles but only an oral Mishnah was available. Actually not a single written copy of the Mishnah is referred to in the Talmud where other books and written documents are mentioned. The silence in the Talmud of a written Mishnah underscores its orality. Oral Torah was delivered only from memory in the course of instruction and debates between rabbis and students and was the basis of all religious education. The fundamental pedagogical element in Jewish education during the rabbinic period was memorization and repetition. Because of the belief in the divine character of the oral and written Torah it logically led to a life long educational principle: a relatively unchanged curriculum, early indoctrination, and a life long pursuit. A good pupil fixed and held in the memory Bible verses, the *halakah* statements, the necessary additions (a sort of Tosefta), an exposition (a sort of Talmud), an indication of its relation to Scripture (a sort of Midrash) and other additional associations, intended to explain and illustrate any rabbinic statement.[146] Let us now trace the importance of memorization in the life of a student from elementary education to the college in the religious Jewish world.

The Student in Preschool in the Rabbinic Period

The term *hinuk* would be considered a sort of pre-school, and points to the purpose of Jewish education of the young boy. As we have already seen the Bible establishes the law to educate your children in Deuteronomy. During the rabbinic period this duty was incumbent upon fathers and grandfathers and applied to sons and grandsons only (Mishnah Kid. 1, 7). As we saw in the biblical period there was a family-like educational structure for early education: the student is a son while the teacher is the father. Usually by the age of three the child had begun to pronounce enough words to begin to memorize. The father was asked to take advantage of the new ability and teach his son to recite from memory two verses from Deuteronomy 6 (b. Hag. 1, 3). The father would teach him gradually the rest of the chapter of the Shema, which was recited from memory every morning and evening. As he would put on the fringes and eat and drink, he learned to say the required *halakahic* sayings from heart. The child lived in an oral world and as we earlier saw from a modern day example this instruction became such a part of the daily routine that he wouldn't even have to try and memorize these commandments they become second nature over time and repetition. An example of the process from moving from the *hinuk* to the Scripture School is given by Maimonides, and though he is outside of our time frame he can still shed light on some principles that likely existed in the rabbinic period, he said in the 12th century: *"The father taught the boy little by little, verse after verse until he was about six or seven, all in accordance with his strength, whereupon he led him to the school teacher."*[147]

---

146. David Carr, *Writing on the Tablet of the Heart* pg. 128
147. Eliezer Ebner, *Elementary Education in Ancient Israel (During the Tannaitic Period)* pg. 22

The home school background in oral and written Torah memorization helped prepare the boy for the first of many stages of a written and oral based Torah education.

The Student in Scripture School in the Rabbinic Period

The Scripture School provided the basic education for boys in reading and memorizing the Torah in the rabbinic period. The boys would first learn the alphabet from memory and then proceed to studying the oral and written Torah. For training their memory pupils were made to learn immensely long passages by heart, and these had to be repeated without an omission, without adding or changing a single word. According to the Talmud school boys were quizzed by adults on their Bible memory verses. Among such answers given were from 1-2 Samuel, Isaiah, Jeremiah, Ezekiel, Malachi and Psalms (Hulin 95b, Git. 56a, Hag. 15a, Ta'an 9b).[148] Portions of the Bible were committed to memory, and then an attempt at understanding was later undertaken. This educational principle, of "learn first and then understand" was practiced within rabbinic Judaism in connection with the study of Torah. The rabbis went so far as to formulate rules for this procedure: *"One should always study the Torah and meditate on it afterwards"* (A. Zar. 19a).

Not only was the oral Torah passed on by memory in the school but so were individual doctrinal statements. There are several passages in the Talmud where a student, or a teacher, consults a rabbi on some doctrinal question or on the wording of some tradition: *"He learned it from him 40 times, and it became for him as though it lay in a purse"* (b. Meg 7b). The doctrinal statement in question was passed on through being repeated several times until the student knew the text by heart. The transmission of oral Torah took place on all educational levels in such a way that the teacher equipped his students with the oral text by repeating it as many times as necessary. This seemingly elementary exercise of repetition was actually accorded more importance the higher up in the school system one goes.[149] By the time the boy left the Scripture School he would have much of the Bible and Mishnah memorized at which point many would often move on to study the Talmud in the college.

The Student in the College in the Rabbinic Period

During the rabbinic period, the college in Israel was usually called *Bet ha Midrash,* in Babylonia the *Bet Rav.* The advanced study might have started at the age of ten or somewhat later depending on the maturity of the student. The origin of the college is obscure, but several texts attest their existence as early as Taanatic times (b. Sabb. 16:1).[150] The procedure adopted by R. Akiva when he arranged and orally published the Mishnah in the 1st century CE was the same method of oral transmission that was still used hundreds of years later in the college. The method was probably something like the following: R. Akiva taught the Mishnah to the first *tanna;* afterwards R. Akiva taught it to the second *tanna* in the presence of the first, then to the third, etc. Subsequently the first *tanna* repeated the Mishnah to the second, to the third etc. Then the second *tanna* recited it to the third, to the fourth and so on.

While descriptions of students repeating their *mishnayot* and *halakhot* from heart are common, such acts of memorization were not ends in themselves. They belonged, rather, to the preparation for the oral

148. ibid pg. 80
149. Birger Gerhardsson, *Memory and Manuscript* pg. 135
150. Samuel Byrskog, *Jesus the Only Teacher* pg. 77

presentation before a rabbi in the college. In this sense, the recitation of rabbinic tradition was not comparable to the recitation by a storyteller. Rather, on the model of rhetorical training students would deliver their memorized texts as part of their larger give and take with teachers and other students.[151]

The Jerusalem Talmud is rich in representations of oral interchanges in which two or more colleagues, or teachers and students, are portrayed in dialogical analysis of memorized texts. In some cases rabbinic disciples were exposed to written materials and might refer to them in case of need. But the overwhelming representation of the Jerusalem Talmud is that resorting to such writings was supplementary to preparation for a learned performance in which such written sources were accessed only through memory.[152]

The principle of literal repetition and memorization of a teacher's words was emphasized and can be seen in a number of passages in the oral Torah. In regards to a *halakah* dealing with the bath of purification Hillel says: *"It is a man's duty to state in his teachers words"* (M. Ed. I.3). The pupil was bound to maintain his teacher's exact wording. But the teacher is also responsible for seeing that the exact wording is preserved. The teacher must repeat it over and over, until he has actually passed it on to his students so they know it by heart. The rabbis formulated educational rules on repetition. The rule of R. Eliezer ben Hyrkanos is said to have been that the teacher had to repeat a doctrinal passage to his pupil four times: *"A man's duty is to repeat to his pupil four times"* (b. Erub. 54b). And when the question of the rabbis' repetition for their pupils is taken up, it is the rabbi who is praised. Thus R. Perida is treated as exemplary; he used to repeat every passage 400 times for a dull pupil, and once when the pupil in question had still not absorbed the passage, he proceeded to repeat it 400 more times. This description gives us a picture of the emphasis on memorization and repetition in the rabbinic college world.

The Student in the Modern Period

Let us now explore what level of importance is laid on memorization in the modern period by obtaining our information directly from students in the yeshiva. I made my way to the Silberstein Yeshiva in the Old City located on the roof of the shouk directly across from the Temple Mount and discussed memorization with a few of the students, one of which named Moshe was of great assistance.

I asked him if he could tell me what is so special about this yeshiva. Moshe said *"Out of all the yeshivas in the world this is one of the very few that is known for its emphasis on memorization of the Torah. We are a dying breed, the yeshiva world does not emphasize memorization anymore but this yeshiva does."* I asked him to tell me what kind of background in memorization does the average student have that attends here. He said: *"Memorization does not start here. In the Mishnah Avoz it tells us how we are to learn. We believe when you are five you should start memorizing portions of the five books at school in the morning and the prophets and writings in the afternoon, even if you don't understand the meaning. When you start the 6th grade you are by now memorizing Mishnah all day every day. The kids are often quizzed by the rabbis on a verbatim recitation and are awarded prizes for accomplishing such feats. The kids memorize by reading the text aloud and repeating it aloud. When you start the 9th grade you start memorizing Talmud."* As we can see Moshe's testimony concerning memorization and the education system of a boy is pretty much

151. Martin Jaffe, *Oral-Cultural Context of the Jerusalem Talmud* pg. 47
152. ibid pg. 50

the same today as it was in the rabbinic period. I then asked him if he could tell me how they review what they have memorized. He said: *"When a student reaches this yeshiva it is up to the individual to review what he has previously memorized, most of us devote an hour or two a day to strictly reviewing. We need to constantly review what we have memorized or else we will forget it. But it is sort of like riding a bike; once you have learned it and done it so many times it becomes second nature. We normally don't review alone. We will find a partner and sit across from each other with our books open but not looking at the written text and take turns telling what we know from memory. We do not do this with the Tenach, only with the oral Torah. If one of us draws a blank then we can look for help from our partner or look down at the text for assistance."* Knowing what the rabbinic sources say about the importance of repeating I asked Moshe what techniques they use to memorize. He said: *"We don't use any special techniques to memorize. Most of what we have memorized is from just repeating it verbally over and over again."* Again we see that the primary memorization tool the students use is verbal repetition.

Also knowing how the Shass Pollak relied on the format of the page as an aid to memorize the entire Talmud I asked him to comment on the format of the printed page and its advantage to memorization. He said: *"The way the text is arranged on the page aids in memorization. The format of the page helps us to remember what is written where and by repetition the page becomes photographed on our minds."* As we earlier saw with the Shass Pollak the format of the page is still a key mnemonic to aid memorization. I then asked him why they memorize particular portions of their texts over others. He said: *"We memorize certain passages in the Talmud and Mishnah more than others because they are more applicable to our daily life. For example we wouldn't emphasize memorizing passages in the Talmud that deal with the sacrificial system in the Temple because it is no longer applicable. We know the Tenach very well but the idea is not to go out to memorize the Bible."* I finally asked Moshe how much do the students at this yeshiva actually have memorized. He said: *"In the yeshiva world very few people know all the Mishnah from memory. Of all the men in our yeshiva about ten know just about the whole Mishnah from heart. Most of the men here know about 90% to 80% of the Mishnah from memory. Almost everyone here knows at least 50% of the Mishnah from heart."* As we have seen from his testimony the emphasis placed on memorization in the rabbinic world today is considerably rare. Moshe pointed out to me numerous times that from his experience very few yeshivas emphasize memorization like the one he attends, and this concurs with R. Shlomo's testimony as well. It is safe to say that your average yeshiva student today would have fundamental prayers, halachik statements and Bible passages memorized but in no way compare to the excellence given to memorization at the Silberstein yeshiva. As Moshe said: *"We are a dying breed the yeshiva world does not emphasize memorization anymore but this yeshiva does."*

The Synagogue in the Rabbinic Period

Let us now consider the emphasis placed upon memorization in the rabbinic period synagogue setting. The synagogue like the school made concerted efforts to facilitate memorization for professionals and lay people alike. In the synagogue the Bible was to be read from the book, despite the fact that the reader usually knew the text by heart. This is the same testimony today. The *targum*, on the other hand, must not be read from the book, but delivered from memory. The translator (*meturgeman*) of the weekly Torah portion from

Hebrew into Aramaic stood alongside the Hebrew reader and translated verse by verse to the congregation. The rabbis forbade his reading the *targum* from a written text, lest the congregation get the false impression that the Torah was originally written in Aramaic. This required the *targum* to recite his translation entirely from memory. Also the Torah reader and the *targum* reader must not be one and the same person; the former might not help the latter with the translation; and the *targum* reader might not begin reciting before the Torah reader had finished (b. Meg. 32a).[153] The weekly or even daily hearing of the spoken Torah would facilitate its memorization to the lay people.

Among the discovered Genizah fragments (T-S AS 67.26) are four examples of *targum* written in shorthand and all on miniature manuscripts. Shorthand texts of the Bible and of the Mishnah, comprising only the first letter of each word or the first word of each verse, were until their finding not known. These were produced in mediaeval times as aides for speaking the memorized *targum*. The reduced size of the *targumic* shorthand manuscripts suggest that they were mnemonic devises prepared by the translator, for inconspicuous use during the reading of the Torah portion in case his memory drew a blank. By referring to abbreviated notes, the *meturgeman* would not technically be violating the rabbinic rule of not reading the *targum* from a book.[154] It was a given that the translator knew the text being read by the *hazzan* from heart and thereby could easily translate it to the audience.

Until the 7th century the tradition of the cantillation of the Torah was handed down orally as we earlier saw was a function of the *tanna*. The rabbis had forbidden the introduction of any signs or markings in the Torah scrolls which meant the entire spoken cantillation had to be memorized verbatim. However, when it became customary to write the punctuated Torah in book form, special signs were introduced to guide the speaker in the proper pronunciation, accentuation and intonation. It was the sages of Tiberias, in the 9th and 10th centuries that perfected the system of vocalization and accentuation. Seeing that there were no markings or vocalization signs in the scrolls from which the public reading of the Torah was made, the readers had to prepare themselves thoroughly via memorization for their oral performance.[155]

The cantor (*hazzan*) had many functions one of which was to lead the congregation in prayer and singing. The qualifications for a *hazzan* in the Talmudic period were: *"one who is meek and is acceptable to the people. Who is skilled in chanting with a pleasant voice, and possesses a thorough knowledge of Scripture, the Prophets and the Hagiographa, who is conversant with the Midrash, Halakhot, and Agadot, and all the Benedictions"* (b. Taanit 16a). In other words these men had to know intimately or have memorized all the oral and written Torah and also had to be able to improvise memorized liturgical texts in accordance with the need of the hour or the occasion. Leading a service became a matter of memory because it was still forbidden at this time to write down prayers: *"those who write down prayers are like those who burn the Scriptures"* (b. Shab. 61b). As the number of prayers grew, it became more difficult to memorize all of them so two men were assigned to stand next to the cantor to serve as possible memory prompters.[156] Just how much the lay people knew from memory by the oral proclamation of the Torah in the rabbinic period we do not know, we may assume many as we have similar records of Jerome's account in the 4th century of

---

153. Birger Gerhardsson, *Memory and Manuscript* pg. 68
154. Michael Klein, *Targumic Texts as Mnemonic Devices* pg. 1
155. Noah Aminoah, *Torah: The Oral Torah* pg. 18
156. Leo Landman, *The Cantor: An Historic Perspective* pg. 5

the lay peoples high knowledge of the memorized word by their continual hearing of the orally proclaimed Scriptures in the Church service.

What was the emphasis on the memorization of liturgy and doctrines in the synagogue setting? R. Akiva wishing to illustrate the way Moses and the people had sung the song at the Red Sea said it was recited in the same fashion as *"the minor who reads the Hallel in the Bet haSefer and the others repeat after him every sentence. R. Jose the Galilean says: as the man who reads the Hallel in the synagogue and the others repeat after him the first part of each sentence."* The teaching of the *Hallel* accordingly proceeded in the following manner. The teacher would recite a sentence in the school and then make the class repeat it verbatim. As soon as the pupils were able to recite the sentence by themselves, the teacher called on individual boys to lead the responsive reading of the group. But while the congregation in the synagogue would repeat only the first part of each sentence, the boys in the Bet haSefer repeated the whole sentence, so that ultimately they should be able to act as cantors of the memorized *Hallel* service in the synagogue.[157]

In regards to memorizing doctrines, certain pupils came to R. Joshua b. Hananiah after having heard a Sabbath lecture given by R. Eleazar b. Azariah (Med. Ad 13.2). R. Joshua asked what new teaching R. Eleazar had given them, whereupon the pupils answered that *"he read this kelal"* (*kelal* is a highly concentrated repetition texts summarizing the message), and proceed to repeat a doctrinal statement, a haggadic midrash consisting of a text of Scripture (Dt. 29:29), a question of haggadic type and an answer supported by Scripture. Later in the conversation the pupils say: *"He also read this kelal,"* after which they repeated a Scripture verse (Jer. 23:7-8) and a parable. Here we see how the students who came from Eleazar b. Azariah's Sabbath lecture memorized a number of his highly concentrated repetition texts, each containing a main point or an important topic from the lecture. The rabbis considered it important to emphasize the main elements in the form of highly concentrated brief repetition texts which were either *halakah* statements, short midrash passages or haggadic sayings of some kind in order to foster memorization of the exact wording of the saying for the benefit of those in attendance.[158]

The Synagogue in the Modern Period

In order to get an authentic understanding of the role memorization plays in the modern day synagogue service I interviewed a professional cantor, Dr. R. Abraham Feder of Jerusalem. I first asked him if the qualifications required for a cantor during the rabbinic period and the role of the *targum* were still applicable today. He said: *"The Talmudic passage relating the requirements of a cantor (b. Taanit 16a) is an ideal statement, and though we would all love to stick to the ideal, that all cantors have such accolades it is not possible in today's world. As for the role of the targum reader most communities do not use one today though some do such as the Yemenites."* I then asked R. Feder to explain the role of memorization in the synagogue today. He said: *"The role of the hazzan is vital to the flow of the service. The greatest mnemonic tool in the synagogue today and at the disposal of the cantor is music and repetition. A melody associated with the text fosters memorization for the cantor and lay people alike. Across the board of the different streams of Judaism today music such as ancient Middle Eastern melodies greatly assists in memorization of the Bible*

---

157. Eliezer Ebner, *Elementary Education in Ancient Israel (During the Tannaitic Period)* pg. 81
158. Birger Gerhardsson, *Memory and Manuscript* pg. 140

and liturgy." I asked him about the role of memorization and young people in the service. He said: *"The familiarity and memorization of the text is ideally taught from early childhood when children memorize the different musical tropes for chanting the Bible and prayers. As a general educational principle memorizing is very helpful for young people and the younger one starts memorizing the better and longer it stays with them. Every bar mitzvah and bat mitzvah requires that the young person memorize how to correctly chant their Torah portion and those who feel led in this direction can receive training to become a professional cantor."* I asked him about the musical patterns used by cantors in the synagogue service today. He said: *"There is a set pattern for musical themes that cantors use. There is a strict pattern recommended for different services. A weekday has one set of musical themes, Sabbath another set, holiday and High Holiday services yet another. These musical patterns experienced over time become familiar with the lay people who can then associate a particular musical melody to a certain text and thereby be more readily able to memorize it."*

I asked him about the memorization of the Bible in the service. He said: *"As part of the liturgy there are biblical texts inserted into the rhythmic liturgy such as the Shema which is recited daily in the prayer service. Because many of the texts are tied to a melody and are repeated so frequently many lay people have portions of the Bible memorized. Memorization is a wonderful system and the best help mate to memorize is putting the biblical and liturgical texts to music. The quantity of Biblical texts chanted by a cantor in the service varies with the different denominations. Orthodox generally read a maximum amount of texts, the reform cut out many of the Biblical texts and the Conservatives are somewhere in the middle. The more traditional the service the more Hebrew texts are spoken. Nevertheless, whatever the denomination or the amount of the texts being chanted music is the key mnemonic feature for memorization in the synagogue."*

Conclusion

As we have seen memorization was emphasized from many angles within the school and synagogue service. It was expected for children to be taught the memorized Torah by their parents in all walks of daily life. The oral recitation of the memorized Torah by the parent was the essential curriculum for the child in the biblical period. In the rabbinic period we saw that a child was expected to memorize the Shema and many of the *halachik* statements before he entered the Scripture School. Once in the Scripture School tremendous emphasis was given to memorizing long passages of the Bible along with the Mishnah and doctrinal statements. At the college level the student could be expected to review continually what he had previously memorized along with now accumulating long memorized portions of the Talmud by the practice of verbal repetition. In the rabbinic period synagogue, the *hazzan* though he read from the text likely had it memorized and the *targum* reader had previously memorized the text in Hebrew and could easily translate it into the common vernacular. The lay people would have learned many passages by heart from their continual hearing and reading of the text in the service, the liturgy was sung with the congregation interacting with the cantor which easily fostered memorization because of their hymnic style, and doctrinal statements were formed by the rabbis in such a way as to make them easy for the congregation to memorize. Finally as we saw from R. Feder the greatest mnemonic tool in the synagogue service today is music accompanied by the chanting of the Biblical text and liturgy. The melody that accompanies the oral proclamation of the text facilitates memorization not only for the cantor but for the lay people alike. Memorization is still alive and well in the world of the synagogue due to mnemonics such as music, but generally speaking memorization within the yeshiva world can be summed up by the student from the Silberstein yeshiva: *"We are a dying breed the yeshiva world does not emphasize memorization anymore."*

CHAPTER VII

Memorization in School
and in the Church Services

In this chapter we want to explore what level of importance was laid upon the student to memorize the Bible and liturgy from the Byzantine and medieval periods up to the modern period. We also want to explore how the Church service facilitated memorization from the early Church through the Byzantine and modern periods.

The Student in the Byzantine Period

Our purpose in this section is not to trace every iota of monastic education; such fine works as *The Love of Learning and the Desire for God* by Jean Leclercq accomplish just that. We know the high importance of education in monastic circles and how they studied a variety of subjects over the ages including the Bible, the Patristic Tradition, grammar, and Classical Literature to name a few.[159] The point I want to communicate is that the monastery was the religious classroom, and the meditation and recitation of memorized Scripture provided all monks with a physical and mental discipline that set the religious tone of every aspect of life. Unfortunately we don't have any sources that tell us about memorization in the religious education process of the Church in the pre monastic movement. Sure we have many sources that we have already quoted that discuss the importance of oral transmission and memorization in the early Church, but there are few if any that combine mentioning memorization and the student other than person "A" heard from person "B". This subject first becomes evident to us textually speaking in the 4th century Rule of Pachomius and his successors who integrated Bible memorization and meditation in all of the monks' daily education or occupations. The monastery was much more than "just" a place of piety and worship but an active, hands on hub of learning and physical labor. The Psalms and other Scriptural passages that the monks were required to memorize as part of their education, were chanted, sung, or murmured aloud not only in formal devotions and communal worship, but during work and leisure, while walking within the monastic compound or traveling abroad, and on special occasions.[160] The meditation on memorized Scripture was the foundation of the monastic education and was especially incorporated into the varied daily labors or education of the monk: farming, gardening, blacksmithing, baking, basket weaving, or whatever: *"At work, they shall talk of no worldly matter, but recite holy things or else keep silent."*[161] And in another place it is written: *"While they were seated on either side of a burning fire, working together at their manual labor and reciting the Holy Scripture by heart a brother appeared."*[162] While many of the particular kinds of manual labor are given

159. Jean Leclercq, *The Love of Learning and the Desire for God* pg. 87
160. William Graham, *Beyond the Written Word* pg. 135
161. *Pachomian Koinonia* 2:156
162. ibid 1:35

attention in the rules of Pachomius, work in the bakery especially emphasizes how they are to combine Bible memorization and meditation with their work. Horsiesius, the disciple of Pachomius, gives regulations which reveal the larger religious purpose of mediating on Scripture during the baking process, a purpose that held for all such meditation during any kind of work or activity: *"When the time has come to make our small quantity of bread, all of us, great and little, must work at making bread in the fear of God and with great understanding, reciting the Word of God with gravity."*[163] The Rule of Pachomius is very specific about how the meditation of Scripture during baking and kneading was to be carried out: *"No one shall speak when the kneading is done in the evening, nor shall those who work at the baking or at the kneading boards in the morning. They shall recite together until they have finished...Let all of us in the kneading room recite, not shouting, but softly...We shall not knead without reciting. We may recite or pause; and if we so desire, we may recite in our heart. If we need a bit of water, we shall strike the trough without saying anything, and those who have charge of supplying water will quickly bring it along. Nor will these cease to recite. No one shall speak when the kneading is done in the evening...They shall recite together until they have finished."*[164] And in another place it is written: *"One works the land as a farmer, another at the bakery, another in the carpenter's shop...And they learn all the Scriptures by heart."*[165]

Beyond their involvement in the more specialized crafts and bread baking, all monks were expected also to engage in the weaving of rushes, both alone in their cells during free time and in company in the daily prayer meetings. The weaved products would then be sold in the laura on Saturday to the public in an open air market setting. Weaving was used especially as a nocturnal labor joined to memorization to help the monks keep the night vigils, since it, like recitation from memory, could be carried out in darkness: *"We always spend half the night...in vigils and the recitation of the words of God, also doing manual work with threads, hair, or palm fibers lest we be overcome with sleep."*[166] And in another place it is written: *"And so, if it happened that the needs of nature compelled him to snatch a little sleep, he would sleep sitting and holding in his hands the ropes he was plaiting. He did not plait the ropes by the light of a lamp, but sitting in darkness, while reciting the Scriptures by heart."*[167] And again: *"Sitting in his cell plaiting ropes and reciting passages of the Holy Scriptures he had learned by heart...would get up and pray every time his heart urged him to do so."*[168]

The education of reciting Scripture was by no means limited to the monks' manual labor alone. The sources reflect the constant recourse to meditation of Scripture encouraged for all occasions. In regards to the role of memorization during meal time it is written: *"The one who strikes the signal to assemble the brothers for meals shall recite while striking."*[169] And in another place: *"The one who dispenses sweets to the brothers at the refectory door as they go out shall recite while striking."*[170] Even such mundane actions as walking and traveling, whether simply between one's cell and the church or other common gathering,

---

163. William Graham, *Beyond the Written Word* pg. 135
164. *Pachomian Koinonia* 2:162
165. ibid 2:129
166. ibid 1:31
167. ibid 2:54
168. William Graham, *Beyond the Written Word* pg. 137
169. *Pachomian Koinonia* 2:54
170. ibid 2:151

between the monastery and the fields or river, or entering or leaving one of the monasteries, was accompanied by the chanting or singing of memorized Scripture. The education of the monastic life consisted of physical labor as well as classroom learning but the backbone of their learning was the Bible and the memorization and recitation of it in every facet of their daily life.

Medieval Period

In the medieval period we have occasional references to the importance of memorizing the Bible, liturgy and biblical facts in a student's education. As a general rule the child was taught to read before being handed over to the monks for further instruction. Seven years was a common age for beginning this elementary study. The child learned his reading mostly from the Psalter. The child learned and memorized both the Psalms and the canticles and was thus prepared to take part in the liturgical services. The Psalms were consigned to memory not only for personal and educational purposes but also for liturgical reasons, for chanting in the services. The instruction in the medieval school was mostly oral. The students got their information by word of mouth from their teachers, rather than from written texts. This is not to assume that written texts did not exist, we have testimony of their usage in the following statements. After his elementary education with its emphasis on memorization, the student could go on to higher studies of which the following quotes concern. The 12th century Christian philosopher and teacher Bernard of Charters' pedagogical techniques are described in the following manner: *"Bernard used also to admonish his students that stories and poems should be read thoroughly, and not as though the reader were put to flight like a spurred horse. Wherefore he always insistently demanded from each one, as a daily debt, something committed to memory."*[171] In regards to memorization and religious textbooks, the preface to the 12th century text *Chronica*, is addressed to young students beginning their study of the Bible in the school of St. Victor. It precedes a chronicle of Biblical history, set out as names, dates, and places, which the students were to memorize as an elementary part of their education in the study of the Bible.[172] Also in the 12th century, Hugh of St. Victor, instructing young students on how to memorize, explains the mnemonic tool of manuscript page layout and decoration which we have also seen emphasized in Judaism. Hugh repeated traditional advice about always memorizing the Bible and liturgy from the same written source to avoid confusion: *"It is a great value for fixing a memory-image that when we read books, we study to impress on our memory...the color, shape, position, and placement of the letters...in what location we saw something positioned...Indeed I consider nothing so useful for stimulating the memory as this."*[173] As we can see from these few sources, even though the Church was living in a printed world they still emphasized the necessity for students to participate in an oral world and in doing so emphasized memorization not only of the Bible but related biblical studies in the medieval period class room.

Modern Period

To get a fist hand understanding of the importance laid on memorization for the student in the modern period, I interviewed students of the Greek Orthodox boy's school in Jerusalem. These teenage boys come

171. Mary Carruthers, *The Book of Memory* pg. 178
172. ibid pg. 81
173. ibid pg. 9

to Jerusalem for a long duration to minister as psaltes in the Church of the Holy Sepluchre as well as receive the equivalent of a high school education. Their curriculum consists not only of standard Western high school classes but also religious classes. Their main function as *psaltes* in the Church is to chant or sing the liturgy and portions of the Bible daily at the Church. The *psaltes* told me that there is not a great emphasis on memorization of the Bible and liturgy in their school though they are required to memorize short portions of the Gospels. In regards to the importance of memorization and their function as *psaltes* in the Church of the Holy Sepluchre they said: *"We always read the liturgy and Bible portions from the text and never quote them from memory at the Church even though we might know some of them from heart. Because we sing certain portions of the Bible and liturgy so many times we thereby know many of them from heart. The assistance of the Byzantine melody to the chanting also helps us in memorization."* They said the reason for not knowing much liturgy from memory is because there is such a vast amount of liturgy and they are still in the formative stages of the ministry of a *psaltes* and thereby are not yet well acquainted enough to have large portions memorized, though they mentioned many 18 year olds do have much memorized. The feeling I got from their testimonies is there is little stress laid on memorization of the Bible in the classroom today, and whatever Bible texts they do have memorized is by default from hearing them chanted over and over in the services. We have to wonder when the emphasis on memorizing the Psalms ceased as a fundamental pedagogical function. We read earlier that Sabas had the Psalms memorized by the age of eight. I am certain the underlying influence of this trend is the Western education model which takes the sap out of memorizing the Bible and instead devotes times to subjects on the periphery of religion and the spiritual life.

I would also like to consider the emphasis put on memorization within the Ethiopian Christian School. The traditional exegesis of the book of Psalms developed by the ancient Ethiopian Church is not a product of the modern period. Rather it has developed over centuries, being handed down by memory through numerous generations from teacher to student, and it is still in our days being taught in the traditional oral way, although this method of oral transmission has been dwindling over the last century.[174] If we were to visit a traditional Ethiopian school any time before the last century, the absence of writing material would be obvious. Eager students would in private write down some notes as a support for their memory, but books and notes were not used in class and the handwritten biblical commentaries such as the Andemta commentary owned by some of the teachers would be few and difficult to find. The study of the Psalms in Ge'ez brings the program of the traditional elementary and high school education to an end. This is because the recitation of David since ancient times has been regarded as a high degree of study and given a much honored place. Since David was seen as the fulfillment of study, all the children made great efforts to pass this step of learning all the Psalms from heart. The Psalms are being recited by the Ethiopians all over the world in the way and order they are studied in the traditional schools of Ethiopia. It is also customary for relatives and friends to bring gifts of congratulation to the new graduate who finishes school with the study (memorization) of the book of Psalms.[175]

---

174. Kirsten Stoffregen Pedersen, *Traditional Ethiopian Exegesis of the Book of Psalms*, pg. 1
175. ibid pg. 14

Memorization and the Church Service
Early Church

What role did speaking the memorized Tenach and the sayings of Jesus have in the 1st century church service? As the early Church in Israel consisted mostly of Jews we can only assume that they continued the synagogue practice of reading the Tenach and translating the *targum* from memory when necessary. That being said what about the oral proclamation of the sayings of Jesus being spoken in the 1st century Church? In order to find the answer let us search for clues in the New Testament. In the prologue to his book, Luke identifies his living sources. Among them are *"the eyewitnesses and ministers of the word"* (Luke 1:2). The single definite article makes it possible that the eyewitnesses and the ministers are one in the same people. A *huperetes* (minister) was the leader of worship in a Greek speaking Jewish synagogue. Luke described this early Christian official as a *huperetes* of the word (of Jesus) not of the synagogue. Three elements are thus brought together to define this oral ministry. First the title for a worship leader in the synagogue is borrowed from Judaism and reused for an early Church minister. Secondly he must be an eyewitness of Jesus and third he is a cantor of the sayings of Jesus. An eyewitness, a leader in worship and an adherent to the sayings of Jesus were selected people to recite the sayings and stories of Jesus from memory in the 1st century Church services in the same fashion a cantor would recite the Bible in the Jewish synagogue.[176] By the oral proclamation of the sayings of Jesus in the Church service the lay people would have the ability to familiarize themselves with and memorize the sayings of Jesus before they were later transmitted into writing.

Oral reading and recitation of Scripture were the primary means through which the Word was heard, memorized and reflected upon in the services. Paul wrote: *"till I come attend to the public reading of Scripture"* (1 Tim. 4:13). Equally clear are references to the public reading of Scripture in the 2nd century in Justin Martyr's *First Apology* and the *Second Epistle of Clement.*[177] Listening to the oral proclamation of Scripture in the early Church fostered memorization for those who heard it proclaimed. For example, Augustine gives testimony to widespread lay familiarity with the memorized Bible. In a letter to Jerome, he criticizes the reading in a service of the book of Jonah in Jerome's new Latin translation. The new version, Augustine complains differs from the text *"which had been rooted in the memory of all the people and repeated in so many succeeding generations."*[178] The lay people knew the book of Jonah from memory because of its being repeated over the years and thereby complained when a new translation that differed from that which they had memorized was used in the service. This phenomenon of memorizing a text by hearing it spoken aloud over and over in the Church service is still prominent today and from all indications it is still the primary means wherewith Christians in the Middle East memorize the Bible.

Byzantine Period

As we move into the Byzantine period Church service let us explore how the preaching and hearing of Scripture facilitated memorization for the audience. John Chrysostom an adherent to the Pachomian Rule's emphasis on memorization in the 4th century employed many mnemonic devices in his preaching meant to

176. *Expository Times vol. 106* pg. 363
177. William Graham, *Beyond the Written Word* pg. 123
178. ibid pg. 124

stimulate the memory of his congregation. Key among these was repetition of the Bible and his messages. John began every sermon with a short recapitulation of the previous one to stimulate the memory. On the structure of his sermons repetition of key phrases and ideas was meant to stamp the exact words into the minds of the listeners. He repeated Bible verses from memory up to seven times within a few minuets of his sermons for a memorable effect. Even with the most optimistic estimation of literacy, not all lay Christians were able to read, but everyone utilized their memories. Chrysostom's instruction in Christian doctrine and behavior depended on reliable memories. According to him the first goal of an ambitious Christian was the memorization and subsequent contemplation of Scripture. He believed that the Bible itself was structured in a way to memorize and was meant *"to rivet the sacred truths in our mind by repetition."*[179] Augustine in the 4th century also had an immense memory for Scripture and utilized it in the Church service: *"In one sermon, he could move through the whole Bible, from Paul to Genesis and back again (from memory)."*[180] The 5th century Greek Church historian Socrates wrote of Atticus, bishop of Constantinople who performed a similar feat: *"Formerly, while a presbyter, he had been accustomed after composing his sermons, to commit them to memory, and then to recite them in church."*[181] It is said of the 5th century Syrian monk Theodore that: *"whenever he spoke to the brothers from the Holy Scriptures of the Lord, he would recite the passages for them and also explain their spiritual significance to them."* In the Byzantine church service passages from the Bible were often quoted without any ascription in sermons (chapter and verse divisions were not to come for another 1000 years); the audience was expected to recognize the source from memory.[182]

Recitation of the Bible from memory can also be seen in the 4th century Tabennesiot monastic community in their twice daily collective prayer meetings. The morning service was held in the common hall with the entire community present, whereas the evening service was held in each house within the compound. The basic form of the church service was repeated rounds of recitation of memorized Scripture and personal prayer. In each meeting, several monks in order of seniority took turns reciting six sections of Scripture before the group, after which all stood and recited the Lord's Prayer from memory in unison.[183] These services were occasions to strengthen the memorization and knowledge of the Bible as well as its interpretation for lay person and monk alike. The basis for everything was the Bible living in the minds and on the lips of those who made its meditation and implementation their chief occupation.[184]

Again one of our best and only sources in the Byzantine Period for the emphasis on memorization in the services comes from the Pachomian community. Reciting previously memorized Bible passages started on the way walking to the service: *"As soon as he hears the sound of the trumpet calling the brothers to the service, he shall leave his cell, reciting something from the Scriptures."*[185] Repeating the Bible from memory also took place in the service itself: *"Among the weekly servers from one house some shall not be chosen to stand on the step and recite something from the Scripture in the assembly of all, but all of them, according to their order of sitting and standing, shall repeat from memory what has been assigned to*

179. Jaclyn Maxwell, *Pedagogical Methods in John Chrysostom's Preaching* pg. 446
180. William Graham, *Beyond the Written Word* pg. 125
181. Mary Carruthers, *The Book of Memory* pg. 207
182. ibid pg. 97
183. William Graham, *Beyond the Written Word* pg. 138
184. ibid pg. 139
185. *Pachomian Koinonia* 2:145

them,"[186] and in another place: *"It was our habit to assemble and for each one to pronounce what he knew of the Holy Scriptures (from memory). That evening when they were seated, each one brought forth the saying he had learned (from heart) or that he had heard from the lips of others."*[187] Memorization also took place after the service ended: *"When the service is dismissed, let us recite until we reach our houses,"*[188] and in another place: *"When the service is dismissed, each one shall recite something from the Scripture while going either to his cell or to the refectory."*[189] The recitation of Scripture provided the fundamental content of formal prayer and worship as well as the core of preaching and teaching in the Byzantine period until the end of the medieval period likely because of the advent of the printing press. Scriptural recitation in the worship service assured the constant presence of the Bible in the mouths and ears of both the clergy and lay people alike.

Modern Period

In the different interviews I conducted with all the different churches in Jerusalem the overriding aid to memorization is the hearing and speaking of the Bible and liturgy in the daily or weekly services. Besides the hearing of and reading of the word in unison there are other techniques used to memorize I would like to consider. In the reading of the liturgy there is a need to frame important information to assist the congregation in memorizing. Let us consider the framing of the passage of Scripture read as the Gospel portion in many services. It is given a frame by the change in the body position of the congregation when they are asked to stand. This may be further enhanced by the procession of the reader to the centre of the people. The frame is extended in sound by a spoken response to the announcement to the reading. On the conclusion of the reading there may be a silence as a time for recall of the key words, and this is followed by another affirmation. All this movement and wording sends out signals about the importance of the words and the need to pay special attention which all foster memorization. [190]Let us also consider the liturgical books used in the Church service. One reason why people are able to remember the words of the Lord's Prayer besides saying it aloud weekly, is that the text on the written liturgy page has been printed in phrase lines, and these are brief enough to be retained in the visual as well as the mental memory. In turn these correspond to the audio memory and so they are able to hear, see and think the Lord's Prayer as they repeat it from memory.[191] As we have earlier read the importance of the page format is of tremendous influence in Judaism and we can see its importance today in the Church service. The Church service today utilizes many devices to instill memorization to those in attendance such as oral proclamation, verbal repetition, bodily position, an orchestrated reading and page layout.

---

186. ibid 2:147
187. ibid 1:53
188. ibid 2:201
189. ibid 2:150
190. Peter Atkins, *Memory and Liturgy* pg. 17
191. ibid pg. 16

Conclusion

It is apparent as we have traced the importance of memorization in the school and church service that tremendous attention was encouraged and devoted to the memorization of the Bible. The Byzantine period testimonies concerning a monastic education are literally teeming with the importance that was given to the memorization and oral recitation of the Bible. It seemed that nothing went on in the monastic life without the accompaniment of the memorized Word. The medieval period sources we have concerning education and memorization also emphasize its fundamental role in pedagogy. The early Church service included the oral rendition of the memorized sayings of Jesus as part of their services. The Byzantine period sources are also teeming with the emphasis put on the oral proclamation of the memorized word in many different ways and means in their services. The modern day Middle East Church service though immersed in a written world still creatively attempts to foster the memorization of the spoken Word into the hearts of those in the audience during the service.

CHAPTER VIII

Techniques Used to Memorize in Judaism

In this chapter we want to explore the different memorization techniques used in Judaism from the biblical, rabbinic, medieval and modern periods. In doing so we want to observe which techniques were unique to which periods and which may have transcended to the other periods. Let us try and get into the mind-set of the ancients and consider the mnemonic tools they had at their disposal to accomplish such great memorization feats.

Memorization Techniques in the Biblical Period
Alphabetic acrostic

The writers of the Bible used such common knowledge as the alphabet as an aid to memorizing portions of the Bible. In an acrostic poem, the first letter of each line follows an alphabetic sequence. A person memorizing such a text would have an easier time recalling the sequence of lines, being able to follow the alphabet memorized first in their primary education. Such acrostics represent one strategy that alphabetic cultures used to cope with the problem of keeping memorized bits of tradition in the correct sequence. The following are some alphabetic acrostics that occur in the Bible: Nahum 1:2-8; Psalms 9; 10; 25; 34; 37; 111; 112; 119; 145; Proverbs 31:10-31; and Lamentations 1-4.

Key Words

Another mnemonic method for unifying individual sections of a text is the idea of putting stress on prominent key words to help the memory. This technique of repetition is characteristic of the oral style and was developed in Hebrew literature into a creative literary device. This form of composition is known in the Psalms, where the recurrence of key words is a basic law of oral style. The repetition of key words enables the listener and reader to provide a thread of continuity which will serve to bind the train of thought together in the process of memorization.[192] For example, there are eight key words in Psalm 119 and most of the lines of the poem contain one of these eight words. The key words are all nouns and generally synonyms:

imra	saying
davar	word
hoq	statute
mitsva	commandment
mispat	judgment
edot	stipulations
piqqud	regulation
torah	instruction, teaching

192. *The Catholic Biblical Quarterly vol. 23* pg.422

Lists

Lists rely on repetitive formulas that the memory appreciates. For example such genealogies as Genesis 5 and 11 use a repetitive list formula to aid memorization.

Meter

Texts constructed in metrical form are more easily committed to memory and are one reason why ancient poetry could be transmitted relatively unchanged over long periods.

Music

Israel had a strong musical tradition, as is attested by the large variety of technical terms associated with music making in the Bible. Although there is no direct testimony that poets recited stories to the strains of music there are psalms of the Bible that clearly state the text was originally supposed to be set to music such as Habakkuk 3. As we know language when sung differs from ordinary spoken language, which in turn affects the traditions of meter.[193] For example: *"They that chant to the sound of the viol, and invent to themselves instruments of music like David"* (Amos 6:5).

Numerical Aids

The ten generations from Adam to Noah, the Ten Commandments or the ten plagues of Egypt are an example of teaching structured for memorization. The ordering of the list into ten items, allows the student to use their fingers to count off and see whether they have counted all of the key points of these fundamental teachings everyone should know by heart.

Numerology

The number eight has an important place in biblical numerology in regards to alphabetic acrostic poems. For example, each stanza of Psalm 119 has eight lines. There are also eight key nouns in the Psalm, corresponding to the eight lines in each stanza of the poem to aid memorization.[194]

Opening Formulas

Another mnemonic device tied together unrelated statements by providing them identical opening formulas to help remember them. An example is found in Amos 1: *"For three transgressions...yea for four."*

Parallelism

A basic feature of biblical songs, sayings, proverbs, etc. is the recurrent use of a relatively short sentence form that consists of two brief clauses. The clauses are regularly separated by a slight pause because the second line is usually a continuation of the first. This kind of style would facilitate the poet's composition of verses and at the same time make memorization easier for the author and audience. The parallel word pair is

---

193. Wilfred Watson, *Classical Hebrew Poetry, A Guide to its Techniques* pg. 92
194. David Noel Freedman, *The Exaltation of Torah* pg. 30

used in the same verse, with one member of the pair in the first line and the second member in the parallel line. For example: *"Like snow in summer and like rain in harvest"* (Proverbs 26:1), and: *"They go up to the sky, they go down to the ocean"* (Psalm 107:26).

Repetition

"Repeat them to your children and recite them when you are at home and when you are away, when you lie down and when you rise" (Deuteronomy 6:7). As we mentioned earlier this text does not refer to discussion or teaching of the interpretation of the words, as is often implied by the translations. Instead it commands a constant process of recitation of the actual memorized words of the Torah during all activities of the waking day. The process envisioned here is one of self and child-Torah education through constant vocal repetition.[195] As we have traced throughout this book verbal repetition was the most facilitated memorization tool in Judaism in all periods.

Rhythm

Rhythm can be described as a recurring pattern of sounds. The mind insists on grouping and highlighting the repetition of identical sounds. The listener is predisposed for rhythmic sequences especially when listening to poetry. Rhythm can be marked by a stress, by loudness, by pitch and by length.

Similar Incidents

To employ a series of similar incidents was also an aid to the memory. An example of this is the stations Israel stopped at during their wanderings after the Exodus: *"And they removed from Elim and encamped by the Red Sea. And they removed from the Red Sea, and encamped in the wilderness of Zin. And they took their journey out of the wilderness of Zin..."* (Numbers 33).

Sing Song

As we know there is no better way to memorize a text than to sing it. The pedagogical connections of Isaiah 28:9-13 are indicated when Isaiah's opponents sarcastically charge him with speaking to them as a teacher speaks to the school child: *"Who will he teach knowledge, and to whom will he explain the message? Those who are weaned from milk, those taken from the breast?"* Isaiah's opponents go on to quote what appears to be a singsong used in an 8th century educational context to facilitate memorization: *"Command to command, command to command, line to line, line to line, a little there, a little there."* The first part of this saying in Hebrew, *tzab latzab, tzab latzab, qab laqab, qab laqab* makes little sense as a statement but more sense as a quote from an instruction. This seeming nonsense phrase is modeled on a pattern of call and response based on the middle part of the alphabet (here *tzade* then *qof*). Following a call-and-response pattern, the teacher would say something like *tzab latzab*, and the students would echo him;

---

195. David Carr, *Writing on the Tablet of the Heart* pg. 137

then the teacher would go on to the next letter of the alphabet. This text provides a picture of an ancient alphabetically based process of call and response to aid the memory.[196]

Song

Some texts depict a process of oral instruction that requires memorization. For example the Song of Moses is instructed to be taught orally to the people: *"Write this song, and teach it to the Israelites; put it in their mouths"* (Dt. 31:19). And in another place David's lament over Jonathan says: *"David ordered that the Song of the Bow be taught to the men of Judah"* (2 Sam. 1:18).

Straightforward Patterns

The function of this pattern among other reasons was to alleviate the process of memorization of the text. An example of this is: *"On every pair of hands (f) a slash (f), on every pair of hips (m) sackcloth (m)"* (Jeremiah 48:37).

Memorization Techniques in the Rabbinic and Medieval Periods

As we mentioned earlier, when we arrive to the time when the oral canon of the Talmud was to be closed there existed numerous techniques to aid in the memorization of the oral and written Torah. Let us investigate some of the popular mnemonics used in these periods and observe if any of the mnemonic techniques used in the biblical period transcended into the rabbinic and medieval periods as well as notice new techniques which fostered memorization.

Biblical Mnemonics

Examples of Bible verses used for a mnemonic purpose in rabbinic literature to aid the memory are numerous. For example, to remember the six orders into which the Mishnah is divided, Isaiah 33:6 was cited: *"there shall be faith in thy times, strength, salvation, wisdom, and knowledge,"* each of the nouns indicates a specific order (b. Shab. 31a). In order to remember the *halachik* rule that basilicas attached to royal buildings are forbidden because of idolatry, but those of baths and storehouses permitted was to be remembered they used the mnemonic: *"to bind their kings with chains"* (Ps 149:8; Av. Zar 16b). The law that if the lungs of animals are liver colored they are permitted, but if flesh colored forbidden had the mnemonic: *"and if flesh in the field, it is terefah"* (Ex 22:30; b. Hul 47b). The mnemonic to remember that one should not curse one's parents in the presence of one's children is the verse Genesis 48:5: *"Ephraim and Manasseh shall be mine even as Reuben and Simeon"* (b. Ket 72b).[197] These *halacha* regulations during the rabbinic period were all based on previously memorized Bible verses helped them remember what to do and what not to do *halachikly* speaking.

---

196. ibid pg. 125
197. *Encyclopedia Judica vol. 12* pg. 187

Brevity

We see the emphasis on brevity not only in ancient Judaism but through the rabbinic period. The tendency was to concentrate teachings and texts, and express them with the utmost brevity is general. We saw this example earlier in the Shabbat lecture given by R. Eleazar b. Azariah (Med. Ad 13.2). There was a very active consciousness of the importance of such concentration, of condensing material into concise, pregnant, and if possible also striking, and succinct sayings to aid memorization: *"A sharp peppercorn is better than a basket of gourds"* (b. Meg. 7a). The well thought out brief statement was the ideal maxim. But the rule enjoining a teacher to teach "in the shortest way" was not primarily intended as a general recommendation to brevity; it was intended to stress the importance of a teacher formulating as concisely as possible the important doctrinal statements: those which were intended as condensed memory texts.[198]

Catchphrases

By their nature these are pithy mnemonic statements in which the element of apparent paradox is often used. To remember that meditating on sin can be worse than its actual commission, the mnemonic was devised: *"the odor of meat"* (i.e. the odor of the meat excites the appetite more than the meat itself).[199]

Image

It was suggested that students form an image of the rabbi who had issued a rule even as they memorized that rule, thus fulfilling the requirement that a rule be cited in the name of its designer (m. Avot 6:6). This was a Jewish version of a Greco-Roman memorization technique from the text *Ad Herennium*. The author, a teacher of rhetoric believed that since sight is the strongest of the senses, the best way to fix something in the memory is to associate it with a place and with objects that can be easily recalled. The author suggests the student mentally walk through a room and fix in their mind the shape of the room and the placement of objects. When the student would memorize a text, they should associate the various ideas of the text with the room and its objects. To recall the speech one would walk through the room and among the furnishings of their mind. The rabbis seem to have used a written text as the Romans a mental room. Paragraphs, words, and letters became keys to memory. The phrases and letters stood for a place and its objects. The places were like tablets or paper, the images like the letters, the arrangement and disposition of the images like the script, and the delivery was like reading.[200]

Initial Letters

Another type of mnemonic consisted merely of the initial letters of words in a list. The best known example is the mnemonic DeZaKH ADaSH BeAHaB for the ten plagues. The Midrash states that it was engraved on the staff of Moses (Ex. R. 5:6). Another example is the mnemonic MaNZePaKh for the letters of the alphabet which have a final form. The medieval grammarians similarly made the mnemonic BaGaD KeFaT for the six letters which take a *dagesh*.[201]

---

198. Birger Gerhardsson, *Memory and Manuscript* pg. 142
199. *Encyclopedia Judica vol. 12* pg. 187
200. Daniel Jeremy Silver, *The Story of Scripture* pg. 214
201. *Encyclopedia Judica vol. 12* pg. 189

Meditation

Meditation is the process by which one ruminates over the memorized word. This process as we earlier saw from Joshua 1:8 is the exercise which causes one to think upon the memorized word and makes one act wisely. The best time for such meditation was considered to be at midnight or before dawn. R. Abraham found allusions for this in such verses as Lamentations 2:19 and Psalm 119:148.[202]

Mnemonics

The word in Hebrew for mnemonics is *siman* (sign). They are memorization devices based on the principle that the mind is able to recall relatively unfamiliar ideas by connecting in some artificial whole parts of them which are mutually suggestive. Many of the mnemonics appear to have originated after the Talmud had been collected and arranged, but was not transmitted to writing. Such aids are employed in the Mishnah, in both Talmuds, as well as by the Geonim and by the teachers of the Torah during the medieval period and today. When the Talmud was finally written down these mnemonic notes were used as a basis for memorization and oral transmission of the Talmud. After its completion the mnemonic signs were retained, since they were of great assistance to many pupils who still had to review and memorize the Talmud. Mnemonics were also invented to indicate the order of succession of the treaties, or of the chapters of individual tractates of the Talmud, as well as for the weekly readings from the Bible. Mnemonics are widely used in the Talmud, as in post-Talmudic literature, but their use in the former was rendered imperative by the fact that the Talmud was originally transmitted orally, and even after it was committed to writing, both the scarcity of the texts, and the preference of teaching the text orally made it necessary for mnemonic devices to be employed. The rabbis laid great store on the efficacy of mnemonics as an aid to study.

R. Hisda in Babylon deduced that the Torah can be acquired only by the use of mnemonics, adducing as evidence the verse *"Put it in their mouth"* (Dt. 31:19). The reason the scholars of Judah retained their learning while those of Galilee forgot it was ascribed to the fact that the former employed mnemonics while the latter did not (b. Eruvin 53a). The mnemonic devices of the Talmud can be divided into two main categories, those in which the mnemonic is an integral part of the text, forming part of its body, and those in which a passage is preceded by the mnemonic as an aid to the memory of what is to follow. Since the essence of the mnemonic is to call to mind the unfamiliar by use of the familiar, it naturally follows that it consists of the use of a well known previously memorized phrases. These phrases can be divided into biblical verses, well known Talmudic phrases, popular proverbs, or readily remembered catchphrases.[203]

Numbers

Numbers were also helpful in memorizing. For example: *"Three things must a man say within his house when darkness is descending on the eve of Sabbath"* (b. Shab 2:7).

Pisuk Ta'amim

To facilitate the task of memorizing the correct reading of the verse and to better recognize its beginning

---

202. Aryeh Kaplan, *Meditation and the Bible* pg. 58
203. *The Jewish Encyclopedia vol. 15* pg. 632

and end, the elementary teacher used a method of intonation, called *Pisuk Ta'amim*. It is a system of musical notes that set the recitation of the text into a rhythmical sequence of chant in accordance with the meaning and meter of the verse. The origin of this system is reported to go back to very early times and its knowledge was transmitted orally (Ned. 37b).[204]

Popular Proverbs

The wealthy Simeon b. Judah ha-Nasi was of the opinion that a certain defect in an animal did not render the animal invalid and he ate its meat, while the poor R. Hiyya discarded it as invalid; they had a similar disagreement about the oil used for the Temple. In both cases a mnemonic was devised into a popular proverb: *"the wealthy are frugal"* (b. Hul 46a).

Repeating Aloud

We frequently see in rabbinic literature the importance that repetition of memorized texts and oral teachings should be carried out in a distinct voice to aid memorization: *"Let your ears hear what you allow to cross your lips"* (b. Ber.13a). We read that R. Judah b. Batyra saw a pupil mumbling and said to him: *"My son, open your mouth, and let your words shine forth"* (b. Ber. 22a). This account was given as a general example of the way in which one of R. Eliezer's pupils repeated in a whisper as a result of which he forgot everything he memorized in three years (b. Erub 54a). The rabbis directly opposed any tendencies towards silent reading and silent repetition. Distinct pronunciation facilitated memorization and facilitated against its being forgotten or distorted.[205]

Review

To aid memorization nothing was found more helpful than frequent reviews. While this is of particular importance to the study of the oral Torah, it applies also to the study of the Bible as we earlier read concerning the Return to Zion yeshiva today. The Talmud waxes eloquent on this subject and illustrates it a number of times. Even to study continuously new subjects without making sure that the old ones are not forgotten, would nearly defeat the purpose. In so doing one would resemble *"a man who sows but does not reap or a woman who bears children and buries them"* (b. Shab. 147b). The Rabbis did not propose any set number of reviews necessary to remember a lesson. As a general rule they believed the more repetitions the better the possibility to memorize. Hillel said: *"You cannot compare one who studies his lesson 100 times to one who studies it 101 times"* (b. Hag. 9b).[206]

Rhetorical Patterns

While discovering the principle behind the cases of the Mishnah, one can memorize the whole by mastering the recurrent rhetorical pattern. Very commonly the syntactic pattern will recur in groups of three or five, or multiples of three or five. The resort to highly formalized language patterns facilitates memorization. The authors so express ideas that a given principle is expressed in a repeated linguistic

204. Eliezer Ebner, *Elementary Education in Ancient Israel (During the Tannaitic Period)* pg. 91
205. Birger Gerhardsson, *Memory and Manuscript* pg. 165
206. Eliezer Ebner, *Elementary Education in Ancient Israel (During the Tannaitic Period)* pg. 93

pattern, with the pattern changing when the topic shifts. The smallest whole units of thought conform to clear-cut patterns. When the rabbis focused upon the smallest whole units of thought a few rules governed. These rules, once memorized, made it easy to reconstruct part of the whole units of thought. Then they dealt with the apodosis of the whole units of thought, the "then…" of the "if…, then…,"construction. The attributives would regularly be followed by words that would recur many times over, always as matched opposites (unclean/clean, prohibited/permitted). Seeing the same pattern hundreds of times and knowing the basic rules made it possible to memorize the entire Mishnah.[207]

Rhythm

Intimately connected with the custom of reading and repeating aloud was the practice of reciting with a rhythmical melody. Rhythm fulfills a pedagogical function: the texts which are learned in this way are memorized and transmitted more exactly than those learned in other ways. A well known saying of R. Johanan reads: *"He who reads the Scriptures without melody and repeats the oral Torah without song, concerning himself the Scripture says: Therefore I also gave them statutes which were not to their advantage"* (b. Meg. 32a).[208]

Sing Song

The Talmud stresses the desirability of memorizing in a sing-song fashion. R. Akiva put it this way: *"a song each day, a song each day."* A different translation is *"sing it, sing it"* (San. 99b).

Superstitions

That superstitions should have accumulated on memorization is to be expected. We read: *"Five things make learning to be forgotten: eating what has been nibbled by a mouse or a cat; eating an animal's heart; regularly eating olives; drinking water in which someone has bathed; and placing one foot over the other when washing them. Five things restore learning to the memory: bread baked on coals; soft boiled eggs without salt; frequent drinking of olive oil and spiced wine; and drinking the water which remains from kneading dough. Ten things are bad for memorizing study: passing beneath the bridle of a camel; and how much more so passing beneath the cattle itself; passing between two women or two camels, or being one of two men between whom a woman passes; passing under a place where there is the foul odor of a carcass; passing beneath a bridge under which water has not flowed for forty days; eating bread not sufficiently baked; eating meat from a soup ladle; drinking water from a conduit which passes through a cemetery; gazing into the face of a corpse"* (b. Horayoth 13b).

Memorization Techniques in the Modern Period

In my interviews with individuals in different streams of Judaism in Jerusalem I have come to the conclusion that there are some methods for memorizing today that have been handed down from antiquity,

---

207. Jacob Neusner, *Oral Tradition in Judaism* pg. 68
208. Birger Gerhardsson, *Memory and Manuscript* pg. 167

but many of the above mentioned methods used during the previous periods are not directly utilized today. The following methods seem to be utilized today.

Hevrutah

A method used in the yeshiva world today is the exercise of finding a *hevrutah* (partner) and memorizing and reviewing together. As mentioned earlier this process includes two individuals sitting across from each other with both having their texts under review open. Each individual quotes a particular portion from memory while not looking at the text. If either one draws a blank they rely either on the written text or their hevrutah to remind them of the memorized text under consideration.

Loci

The classical method of mnemonics called loci (method of locations) was first described in Roman books on rhetoric. We saw this method used in the 20th century by the Shass Pollak. When using the method of loci, the Shass Pollak pre-memorized the images of the Talmud in a sequence of previous locations. Each word of the Talmud is associated to its corresponding location using visual imagery mediation. The important point is that the loci organize information by providing a ready-made memory structure for it, and within the structure are a number of places, like distinctive containers, for the items of information to be stored. This process allows the words to be recalled in a specific order. The method of loci not only enables a great deal of information to be recalled, but imposes a serial organization of it.

Public Reading

The most utilized technique of memorizing today is by the often heard public reading of the prayers and Torah in the daily synagogue service whereby spoken written texts become hidden in the heart of the hearer by their constant exposure. By hearing and reading the same portions so many times, for year after year there develops a familiarity and degree of verbatim memorization.

Song

In the world of the synagogue the best available mnemonic is the song. Such biblical texts or prayers put to music increase the ability for that text to be memorized by the audience.

Verbal Repetition

Another method is similar to the song but different; consistent verbal repetition. I would consider this exercise more individualistic than communal. This same exercise so prevalent in the rabbinic period is still considered today to be the most reliable and utilized tool for memorizing Torah in Jewish thought and practice.

Conclusion

Lying underneath the surface of the oral and written Torah are numerous mnemonics deliberately designed by the authors to aid the hearer or reader in memorization, and are not usually evident in translations. Not only did the words and format of portions of the Torah aid in memorization but the Jewish people developed over the millennia scores of mnemonic techniques to facilitate memorization. These memorization aids helped place the oral and written tradition on the forefront of the minds of the Jewish people and assisted them in transmitting their oral tradition for ages. As we have seen there were numerous mnemonic techniques available to memorize in Judaism over the ages. Some of the techniques were more difficult than others and required a previous knowledge of the memorized written Torah to facilitate them. Yet others were quite simple in nature and would be available to implement by any person. Of the over thirty memorization techniques I have listed, which is by no means exhaustive, we can glimpse the admiration that the oral world of Judaism put on the memorization and recitation of the oral and written Torah during all periods.

CHAPTER IX

Techniques Used to Memorize in Christianity

Like in the previous section we want to explore the different memorization techniques used to memorize but in this case in the Church from the early period, Byzantine, medieval and modern periods. In doing so we want to observe which techniques were unique to which periods and which may have transcended to other periods. Let us try and get into the mind-set of the ancient Christians and consider the mnemonic tools they had at their disposal to accomplish such great memorization feats.

Memorization Techniques in the Early Church

For most people during the early Church, a scroll was a commodity that one heard through the medium of another human voice; 'reading' was the activity of orally proclaiming a text before an audience in a social setting.[209] As we have seen the practice of verbal repetition was the fundamental hallmark of memorization in antiquity. There were also other techniques that the early Church used to memorize. Reading a text that had imbedded mnemonic aids helped the audience to be able to memorize the text being spoken. For example let us consider the many imbedded memorization aids in the Apocalypse that would have made the book more immediately understandable and memorizable to the audience. The book can be spoken aloud in one hour, I know this from experience because I have memorized the book and have spoken it publicly many times. John meant for the audience to retain the structure of the book in their memory during the recitation. John provides a great deal of mnemonic assistance, and many would be able to grasp its basic shape in a few hearings. The audience cannot help but notice the lists of sevens that John provides as memory hooks. These septets take the listener almost through the whole book: seven churches, seven seals, seven trumpets, seven bowls. These numerical techniques provide landmarks to enable the speaker and audience to keep their mental bearings.[210]

Another mnemonic technique John used to assist the memory is place and image. Anyone familiar with the geography of Asia Minor would have had no problem keeping the seven churches in geographical order, for they are presented in order beginning at Ephesus and proceeding in a circle along the Roman road. Also the content of each letter is related to the physical setting to which it is addressed. For example, Ephesus, twice forced to move because of the silting of the port, is threatened with the removal of its lamp; and this home of Artemis, Goddess of life and symbolized by a tree, promises those who overcome to eat of the tree of life. Smyrna itself was destroyed and rebuilt, and is addressed by the one who died and came to life. Ten days of tribulation are predicted for this city which is home of the Rites of Niobe, rites which include ten days of mourning. Pergamum, the earliest and greatest center of the Imperial Cult, dwells where Satan's throne is. Thyatira, known for its commerce, is charged with doing commerce with idols. Sardis a nearly impregnable

---

209. P.R. Ackroyd, *The Cambridge History of the Bible vol. 1* pg. 48
210. David Barr, *The Apocalypse of John as Oral Enactment* pg. 244

city that was twice conquered through surprise nighttime attacks is warned that Christ will come like a thief in the night. Philadelphia, with its large Jewish community, is addressed by the one who has the key of David. Laodicea a city of tepid water is rebuked for its lukewarm religion; specializing in the production of rich black wool, they are offered white robes; famous for its eye salve, they are taunted for their blindness. John is talking to the audience in language they understand, and these places and their associated histories are memorization devices which would enable the hearer to keep their order and message in scope.[211]

It is as the listener of Revelation leaves the majority of numeric structuring that place takes on more significance as a mnemonic. The mental gaze is directed in a descending and ascending pattern: first to the sky, then to earth and sea, followed by the mountain and temple in heaven. With each place a dominant image is associated to help the memory: woman and dragon with sky, beast with earth and sea, lamb with the mountain, and one seated on a cloud with the temple. The sequence of places and images are strong enough to allow the listener to remember the associated actions. From the temple proceed the angels with the seven bowls, who then present two more place-images: they show the harlot seated on seven hills and the bride viewed from the mountain. This marked sequence of place and images are to provide images for the memory and would allow the attentive hearer to fix the scope of the action of the book in memory. The Apocalypse is an example of an early Christian literary work intended for memorization and repeated oral performances.[212]

Memorization Techniques in the Byzantine and Medieval Periods

It is not until we arrive at the Byzantine and medieval periods that we discover a plethora of specific techniques that describe how Christians actually went about to memorize. Our knowledge of many of these mnemonic techniques comes from inferences in the related sources, there was not a *How to Memorize* book in antiquity, the information was passed on orally from generation to generation.

Architectural Mnemonic

In medieval Christianity, the passage from 1 Corinthians 3:10-17 became the authority for a fully developed mnemonic technique, using the plans of a building laid out in one's mind as the structure for memorization. The notion follows the idea that you are God's temple and the inventive work of building its superstructures is entrusted in your memory. Students are to use the mental building they have laid out on the foundation of their knowledge of the Bible as a structure in which to gather all the bits of subsequent learning.[213]

Backwards and Forwards

One accomplishment greatly admired by ancient and medieval scholars was the ability to recite a memorized text backwards as well as forwards, or to skip around in it in a systematic way without becoming lost.[214]

---

211. ibid pg. 245
212. ibid pg. 246
213. Mary Carruthers, *The Craft of Thought* pg. 20
214. Mary Carruthers, *The Book of Memory* pg. 18

Brevity

The idea that memory requires brevity is a basic technique we have seen numerous times. The first task of memorizing was to divide a text up into brief portions. In order to remember a long text one divided it into sections that respect the length of short term memory or as the medieval writers said: *"what the mind's eye can take in at a single glance."*[215] For example, several prayers by Anselm of Bec in the 11th century are examples of how brevity fosters memorization. The prayers were to be taken a little at a time and pondered slowly. For ease of meditation, Anselm took care to divide the prayers into memory sized pieces.[216]

Chapter and Verse

The late medieval Bible is divided into numbered chapters to help foster memorization; this format is called the Paris Bible. The 13th century inventor of this format, Stephen Langton, wrote: *"by divisions, that is by chapters…which truly are most valuable for discovering what you want and holding it in your memory."*[217] It was the universal custom in early medieval Church services and scholarly composition not to use numbers at all when citing Biblical sources the reader was expected by memory to know where the passage was found.

Circumstances

Hugh of St. Victor in the 12th century stressed the need to impress the circumstances during which a text was memorized as part of the associational web needed to recall it: the sort of day it was, how one felt, and so on.[218]

Concentration

The 13th century biographers of Thomas Aquinas associated his deep concentration with his remarkable memory: *"Whenever he read in the Sacred Books, and something was once tossed into his mind, he indelibly wrote it in his heart. He had a memory for whole books because having heard something once he took it not idly, but with continued devout attention his emotion-memory chewed on it."*[219]

Hook Words

A deep impregnation with the Bible explains the extremely important phenomenon of reminiscence, whereby phrases excite the memory that a mere allusion would evoke a scriptural phrase elsewhere in the Bible. As one who has been memorizing for many years this happens quite often. For example, the other day I was reviewing Psalm 2, *"ask of me and I will give you the heathen for thy inheritance, and the uttermost parts of the earth for your possession."* And immediately in my memory I associated the phrase *"the uttermost parts of the earth"* with the Great Commission in Matthew 28, *"you will be my witnesses in Jerusalem, Judea, Samaria, and to the uttermost parts of the earth."* What the theological connection is if

---

215. Mary Carruthers, *The Craft of Thought* pg. 63
216. ibid pg. 103
217. Mary Carruthers, *The Book of Memory* pg. 97
218. ibid pg. 60
219. ibid pg. 174

any is a different matter. Each word is like a hook, it catches hold of one or several others which become linked together and make up the fabric of the text. Hearing words similar to other words sets off a chain reaction of associations which mentally cross-references words throughout the Bible that have no more than a chance connection with one another.

Illuminated Books

The Codex Alexandrinus, a 5th century Greek Bible, has a drawing of an empty vase into which an inscription issues as though in a stream. This image serves as a reminder that the Word of God is to pour forth as a stream from the book into the vessel of the memory, and that one's task is to be sure they are diverted there properly. [220] A 15th century memorization text gives advice to pay attention to the color of lines and the appearance of the page in order to fix the text as a visual image in memory: *"one best learns by studying from illuminated books, for the different colors bestow remembrance of the different lines and consequently of that thing which one wants to get by heart."*[221]

Imagination

Peter of Celle in the 12th century suggested imaginatively walking through Scripture in your mind to foster memorization: *"In the book of Genesis journey through the greater part of your reading, coming to paradise. Walk with God, like Enoch. Enter the Ark at the time of the Flood. Go with a deliberate but light step through the contents of this book. Interpret what is obscure, retain and memorize what is straightforward."*[222]

Meditation

An almost ceaseless practice of recitation was enjoined upon all members of monasteries in all periods, and this recitation and constant internalization of Scripture were the overriding goals of memorization. The general rule of thumb was *"Recite constantly the words of God."*[223] Memorization and meditation were thought of as food, involving preparation, digestion and excretion. John Cassian in the 4th century likens the mind thinking to a mill-wheel grinding flour similar to the statement *"garbage in, garbage out."* John said: *"The exercise of meditation is not inappropriately compared to that of a mill which is activated by the circular motion of water. The mill cannot cease its operations at all so long as it is driven round by the pressure of the water, and it then becomes quite feasible for the person in charge to decide whether they prefer wheat or barley to be ground. And one thing is clear. Only that will be ground which is fed in by the one who is in charge. If we turn to the constant meditation of Scripture, if we lift up our memory to the things of the Spirit, then the thoughts deriving from all this will be spiritual."*[224]

---

220. ibid pg. 247
221. ibid pg. 9
222. Mary Carruthers, *The Craft of Thought* pg. 109
223. *Pachomian Koinonia* 3: 17
224. Mary Carruthers, *The Craft of Thought* pg. 91

Meditative Prayer

Monastic rhetoric developed an art for composing prayer that conceives of composition in terms of making a way among places. These places took the form of short memorized Bible verses. The steps were commonly applied to the emotional route that one would take in their course of such composition from fear to joy. The steps were always characterized as routes through the things in one's memory.[225]

Mental Compartments

To learn all the Psalms from heart one first constructed a series of mental compartments, numbered from 1-150. To each number was attached the first few words of each Psalm, so that as one visualized the number one, they simultaneously visualized: *"Blessed is the man that walks not in the counsel of the ungodly."* This scheme has a rigidly ordered background as a grid which is then filled with images.[226]

Murmuring

Reading is often memorized with the aid of a murmur, mouthing the words as one turns the text over in one's heart. It is this movement of the mouth that established rumination as a basic metaphor for memorial activities. The reader usually pronounced the words with his lips, at least in a low tone and consequently heard the sentence seen by the eyes. This results in more than a visual memory of the written words but a muscular memory of the lips. We remember in Augustine's *Confessions* how shocked he was to see someone reading without moving his lips. What resulted was a muscular memory of the words pronounced and an aural memory of the words heard. Of John of Gorze from the 10th century it was claimed that the murmur of his lips pronouncing the Psalms resembled the buzzing of a bee.[227] This was not a silent, interior act of mind and heart alone, the tongue had also to be involved. Meditation denotes an oral activity, namely, to murmur, recite or repeat aloud from memory. One moves one's mouth vigorously, chewing the words of the text, savoring them and working through them to extract all of their spiritual nourishment. What the mouth repeats, the heart should experience, the mind grasp, and the whole being translate into practice.

Numbers

Numbers were also used as mnemonic hooks. For example; the seven deadly sins, the eight Beatitudes, and the Ten Commandments could all be counted on the fingers.

Ornaments

Ornaments were used to help facilitate memorizing a text. Many of the basic features of the ornaments are also elementary principles of mnemonics: surprise and strangeness, exaggeration, orderliness and pattern, brevity, copiousness, similarity, opposition and contrast. All of these characteristics make the text richer and nourishes the mind engaged in memory work.[228]

---

225. ibid pg. 60
226. Mary Carruthers, *The Book of Memory* pg. 82
227. Jean Leclercq, *The Love of Learning and the Desire for God* pg. 89
228. Mary Carruthers, *The Craft of Thought* pg. 117

82

Physical Posture

Physical posture was thought to induce the mental concentration necessary for memory work. For example, Thomas Aquinas would lie face-downwards when memorizing. Lying down was not the only posture: sitting or standing at lectern pensively, head in hand or staring into space, eyes open or closed, with or without a book were also common postures of meditative memory work. Posture and space were thought to be significant because they help to prepare a mental attitude and mood necessary for memorization.[229]

Superstitions

That superstitions were to arise in their oral world is to be suspected. Drunkenness is especially bad, but so are all sorts of immoderate activities for memorization. A diet which includes fatty meats, strong wine, vinegar and all sour things were also considered bad for the memory. Certain herbs, especially ginger were considered beneficial as well as bathing one's head in an herbal concoction every ten days.[230]

Topographical Arrangement

In the 12th century, Peter of Celle advised that one should by progression run through the 42 stopping places in the book of Numbers with what they theologically signify. The stopping places served as a compositional mapping structure. Each location would be labeled by the name of a virtue arranged in sets of six or seven each. Then into each set a theological significance can be collected. In this way, the 42 places were made to serve as a topically arranged collection of virtues convenient for all kinds of later use.[231]

Virtue

Memorization was one of the five divisions of ancient and medieval rhetoric; it was considered to be the noblest of all and the basis for the rest. Memorization was also an integral part of the virtue of wisdom. Training the memory was much more than a matter of providing oneself with the means to compose and converse intelligently when books were not at hand, for it was in trained memory that one built character and judgment.[232]

Writing

Writing was thought to be a memory aid, not a substitute for it. Writing itself was judged to be an ethical activity in monastic culture. A 12th century sermon says: *"Let us consider then how we may become scribes of the Lord. The parchment on which we write for Him is a pure conscience, whereon all our good works are noted by the pen of memory."*[233]

Memorization Techniques in the Modern Period

As we come to the section considering mnemonic techniques in the modern period we are almost

229. ibid pg. 174
230. Mary Carruthers, *The Book of Memory* pg. 50
231. Mary Carruthers, *The Craft of Thought* pg. 110
232. Mary Carruthers, *The Book of Memory* pg. 9
233. ibid pg. 156

totally limited to retrieving our information from living persons. In order to get an understanding of the memorization techniques used by the Church in the Middle East today I asked particular persons within the different denominations of the Church in Jerusalem to explain how they memorize.

Copts

From my interviews with members of the Coptic Church I discovered the great emphasis they have on memorization of the Psalms and liturgy, as well as some of the mnemonic techniques they use to memorize today. The main techniques used to memorize are the constant oral and aural exposure to the Bible and liturgy being read aloud in the daily services. It is from hearing and reading the text so many times that they memorize the text. As a help to the memory they will occasionally glance at the first word in a particular portion of their liturgy in order to help stimulate their minds of the previously memorized portion. Father Dumadius showed me an example of this technique. He retrieved one volume of the liturgical book *Holy Songs of Midnight*. He then opened the book to see the first word of the liturgy and then closed the book and with lightning speed rattled off the liturgy from memory without effort. The volume he was holding had 437 pages of which he said many monks know by heart. As far as I could tell the Copts do not use any of the mnemonic techniques used in the Byzantine and medieval periods except that of being exposed to the daily oral and aural presentation of their texts in the daily services. The technique of using the first word in the text to stimulate the memory is certainly ancient but I have found no previously recorded instances of this mnemonic technique.

Armenians

From my interviews with members of the Armenian Church I discovered that they facilitate no unique mnemonic aids for memorization. Father Gomidass told me that they like the Copts use the aspects of continual hearing and reading from their daily services as techniques to indirectly foster memorization. Other than the oral and aural daily exposure to the texts they don't use or know of any other memorization techniques to facilitate memorization. Father Kousan also of the Armenian Church told me the memorization techniques used today by Armenians are reading and repeating the text aloud. Father Kousan said: *"In the Armenian Church memorization is an individual aspiration, there is no special focus on memorization within the Church on any level."* The ancient method of verbal repetition is still the predominant technique used for memorization across the board today in the East.

Syrians

From my interviews with members of the Syrian Church I discovered that they like the Copts and Armenians rely mostly on the oral and aural exposure of texts in their daily services to foster memorization. Father Shimon told me that through repetition, reading, praying, singing, and hearing texts so often they become memorized. As we see both oral and aural repetition are the linchpins in memorization today in the Middle Eastern Church. One technique mentioned by the Syrians was the emphasis put on the sing song rendition of texts in order to make them easier to memorize.

Ethiopians

From my interviews with members of the Ethiopian Church I recognized there is a tremendous emphasis on the monks to memorize the Psalms and liturgy. This memorization feat is carried out in many ways. First like all the other Churches the daily oral and aural exposure to the spoken Word fosters memorization. But unlike the other Churches I found that the Ethiopians devote significant time daily to finding a partner and reviewing the memorized text together. The pair sits together with one book open and usually the younger monk reads aloud at lightning speed from Dawid and the older monk corrects his pronunciation when needed. There is an intentional and rigorous devotion to orality and memorization today in the Ethiopian Church.

Greek Orthodox

From my interviews with members of the Greek Orthodox Church I discovered that they like almost all the other Churches in Jerusalem do not use any specific techniques like we saw previously listed during the Byzantine and medieval periods to memorize. There is nothing to be found in all my interviews of any special techniques except that of verbal repetition. This should not surprise us though since this technique as our sources have shown was the most favored method to memorize in antiquity. Memorization by repetition is encountered in at least two arenas. The first is in the service by the daily repetition of the Bible and liturgy as has been previously mentioned. The second is by the verbal repetition the monk would perform of the Bible and liturgy in his own time.

Latins

From my interviews with members of the Latin Church I discovered that they like the Copts, Armenians and Syrians rely mostly on the oral and aural exposure of texts in their daily services to memorize. Father Maier told me they memorize both by hearing and reading the texts so many times in the daily services. Like the other denominations mentioned so far he mentioned that many of them do not strive with the specific intent to memorize specific portions of the Bible and liturgy but from the constant oral and aural exposure it comes quite naturally by reason of repetition. Like the Syrians, the Latins told me they find that the oriental liturgy is much easier to memorize because it is accompanied to a hymn, to singing.

Conclusion

As we have read, the authors of the Bible placed a tremendous emphasis on the memorization of the Bible by including in their written transmission mnemonic techniques that would foster memorization for those who heard that text being read. We saw the numerous aids to memorization John includes in the Apocalypse. During the Byzantine and medieval periods we saw over twenty different mnemonic techniques that made the memorization of vast amounts of Scripture possible. Many techniques are still applicable today to those who have the courage to try. We saw from the numerous interviews from the different Churches in Jerusalem that the most utilized tool in memorization today is the same ancient tool that has been stressed over and over again in this book, verbal repetition. Whether the exercise of repetition comes from participation in the Church service or through private devotions it is the favored way of memorizing in the East.

EPILOGUE

From my research I believe that many have ceased to recognize one of the main purposes for which Scripture has been bestowed upon mankind. That purpose is given in Joshua 1:8: *"this book of the Torah shall not depart out of your mouth but you shall meditate on it day and night, that you may observe to do according to all that is written in it, then shall you make your way prosperous then you shall have good success."* The reason is to memorize the exact words of the Bible and then meditate on the exact wording day and night in order to produce a life of obedience and faith. But memorization has been forgotten in the 21st century, or else deliberately ignored, primarily because of the apathetic disposition shown towards it and the difficulties and discipline to be overcome in putting it into daily practice. The idea of an oral characteristic of Scripture has been shattered today, by means of constantly repeated blows from the pulpit to the classroom. The edifice of the memorized building of which so much time and care had been spent by our brothers and sisters from antiquity is relatively non-existent today. The poor effort given to memorizing the Bible from leaders, teachers and parents has in part snatched from the hearts of our future leaders their most important weapon, the memorized Word.

There are certain truths which stand out openly on the roadsides of life, as it were, that everyone may see them. Yet because of their very obviousness, the general run of people disregard such truths or at least they do not make them the object of any conscious knowledge. People are so blind to some of the simplest facts that they are highly surprised when somebody calls attention to what everybody ought to know: *"hide God's word in your heart and meditate on it day and night."* To eliminate the causes of such a development is an action that surely well deserves our attention today. The struggle to influence others to hide God's word in their heart must be carried on with the only weapon that promises success, the power and example of the spoken divine Word.

The message of this book has always emphasized the same conclusion. The leading slogan was illustrated in many ways and from several angles, but in the end we always returned to the assertion of the same formula; Judaism and Christianity have almost always adhered to the orality and memorization of Scripture. Once people recognize the importance of memorizing the Bible and begin the journey of memorizing, they will be rewarded by the surprising and incredible results that such a persistent spiritual discipline produces. And although the ability or desire to memorize the Bible is disappearing more and more today in the younger generation, owing to the all pervading influence of the world, yet among the younger generation there is a remnant who are willing and able to maintain themselves in this most important spiritual practice though they are surrounded by others who look on it apathetically.

The possibility of success in the use of this spiritual weapon consists in the mass employment of it in all spheres today, and when employed it shall bring full returns for the large expenses, efforts, and dedication it incurred. It may be unpleasant to dwell on such truths, but if something is to be changed we must start by diagnosing the disease. The journey we have taken through this book has clearly shown the emphasis and necessity that was placed upon memorizing the Bible over the ages in Judaism and Christianity. They gave a great deal of excellent and practical encouragement to memory, especially up to the modern period. Our present age certainly has nothing of equal worth.

The force which has ever and always set in motion great historical revivals of religious movement is the power of the spoken word. The broad masses are more amenable to the appeal of the spoken than to the written word. These oral movements are the volcanic eruptions of human passions and emotions, stirred into activity by the torch of the spoken word cast into the midst of the people. The staleness of a religion can be averted only by a storm of glowing passion one person at a time; but only those who are passionate themselves can arouse passion in others. It is only through the capacity for passionate feeling that we can wield the power of the memorized divine Word which, like hammer blows, will open the door to the hearts of the people through our example.

We must be restored to memorization of the Bible, now. Even if the practice were to be disadvantageous from an economic standpoint, still it ought to take place. The plough is the Word, and the tears of labor will produce the daily bread stored up in the hearts both of the one who memorizes and of others. The struggle for memorization should be waged in its bitterest form around the home and school of all levels, because this is the nursery where the seeds must be watered which are to spring up and form the godly next generation. The tactical object of the fight is winning over the minds of those who have ears to hear.

For thousands of years the memorized word has been the faithful companion of man and has helped him lay the foundations of spiritual progress, but now the written word has dispensed with the use of the oral. The achievements of Judaism and Christianity provide the basis on which the struggle for daily life was carried on in the Middle East and must be carried out every where in the world today. They provide the necessary example and instruments for our struggle to change people's way of thinking about the importance of memorizing the Word of God: *"Thy word have I hid in my heart, that I might not sin against thee"* (Psalm 119:11).

BIBLIOGRAPHY

Ahlstrom, G.W. *Oral and Written Transmission Harvard Theological Review vol. 59* (MA: Harvard Press, 1966) Pages 69-81

Alan Kirk; Tom Thatcher, *Memory, tradition, and text: Uses of the past in early Christianity* (GA: Society of Biblical Literature, 2005)

Alexander, Elizabeth Shanks *The Orality of Rabbinic Writing: The Cambridge Companion to the Talmud and Rabbinic Literature* (Cambridge: Cambridge Univ. Press, 2007) 1-223

Aminoah, Noah *The Oral Torah: An Outline of Rabbinic Literature Throughout the Ages* (Jerusalem: World Zionist Press, 1994) Pages 1-176

Atiya, Aziz *A History of Eastern Christianity* (London: Methuen Press, 1968) Pages 1-68

Atkins, Peter *Memory and Liturgy: The Place of Memory in the Composition and Practice of Liturgy* (VT: Ashgate Press, 2004)

Attridge, Harold W. *Psalms in Community* (Atlanta: Society of Biblical Literature, 2003). Pages 7-32, 341-356

Bailey, Kenneth *Jesus Through Middle Eastern Eyes* (IL: IV Press, 2008) Pages 11-21

Bailey, Kenneth *Middle Eastern Oral Tradition and the Synoptic Gospels: Expository Times vol. 106* (Edinburgh Press: 2000) Pages 363-367

Bailey, Kenneth *Poet and Peasant and Through Peasant Eyes (MI: Eerdmans Publishing, 1984) Pages 30-43*

Barr, David *The Apocalypse of John as Oral Enactment: Interpretation vol. 40* (1986) Pages 243-256

Bartholomew, Gilbert *Feed my Lambs: John as Oral Gospel* (GA: Semeia vol. 39 Scholars Press, 1987) Pages 69-96

Bjork, Robert *Memory* (NY: Academic Press, 1996) Pages 348-374

Booth, Wayne C. *The Craft of Research* (IL: University of Chicago Press, 1995)

Bradshaw, John *Oral Transmission and Human Memory Expository Times vol.92* (1980), p.303-307

Buxbaum, Yitzhak *Storytelling and Spirituality in Judaism* (NJ: Northvale, 1994) Pages 5-81

Byrskog, Samuel *Jesus the Only Teacher* (Coniectanea Biblica NT Series vol. 24) Pages 55-77, 156-159, 228-235

Byrskog, Samuel *When Eyewitness Testimony and Oral Tradition Become Written Text: Svensk Exegetisk Arsbok vol. 74* (IL: ATLA Press, 2009) Pages 41-53

Carasik, Michael *Theologies of the mind in Biblical Israel* (NY: Lang: Press, 2006)

Carr, David McLain, *Writing on the tablet of the heart: origins of Scripture and literature* (Oxford: Oxford University Press, 2005)

Carruthers, Mary *The Craft of Thought* (NY: Cambridge Univ. Press, 1998)

Carruthres, Mary *The Book of Memory* (NY: Cambridge Univ. Press, 1990)

Childs, Brevard S. *Memory and Tradition in Israel* (IL: Allenson Press, 1962)

Chilton, Bruce *A Galilean Rabbi and His Bible* (UK: SPCK Press, 1984) Pages 35-56

Cohen, A. *Every Man's Talmud* (London: Dent and Sons Publishing, 1968)

Coxe, Cleveland A. *The Ante-Nicene Fathers* (MI: Eerdmans Publishing, 1979)

Culley, Robert C. *Oral Formulaic Language in the Biblical Psalms* (Belgium: Univ. of Toronto Press, 1967) Pages 3-20

Cuthbert, Lattey *The Place of Memory in the Composition of the Synoptic Gospels vol. 1* (Biblica, 1920) Pages 327-340

Dana, H.E. *The Ephesian Tradition* (MO: Kansas City Seminary Press, 1940) Pages 11-27

Draper, Jonathan A. *Orality, Literacy, and Colonialism in Antiquity*
(MA: Brill Press, 2004) Pages 37-63, 83-91, 135-151, 193-217, 248-269

Ebner, Eliezer *Elementary Education in Ancient Israel During the Tannaitic Period*
(NY: Bloch Publishing, 1956) Pages 1-95

Elman, Yakkov, Gershoni Israel *Transmitting Jewish Traditions: Orality, Textuality,
and Cultural Diffusion* (London: Yale University Press, 2000)

Encyclopedia Judaica vol. 12 (Jerusalem: Keter Publishing, 1971) Pages 187-190

Eusebius, *The Ecclesiastical History* (MA: Harvard Press, 1992) Pages 1-400

Freedman, David *Noel Psalm 119 The Exaltation of Torah* (IN: Eisenbrauns Press, 1999)
Pages 25-55, 77-80

Gerhardsson, Birger *Memory and Manuscript* (Copenhagen: Munksgaard Press, 1961)

Gerhardsson, Birger *The Secret of the Transmission of the Unwritten Jesus Tradition
New Testament Studies vol. 51* (January 2005) Pages 1-18

Gerhardsson Birger *Tradition and Transmission in Early Christianity* (Gleerup: Lund Press, 1964)

Gizenberg, Louis *The Legends of the Jews vols. 1, 3, 4*
(PA: The Jewish Publication Society of America, 1909)

Goitein, S.D. *A Mediterranean Society Vol. 2* (CA: Univ. of California Press, 1971) Pages 198-211

Goodspeed, Edgar *An Introduction to the New Testament* (IL: Univ. of Chicago Press, 1944)
Pages 125-131

Graham, William *Beyond the Written Word: Oral Aspects of Scripture in the History of Religion*
(NY: Cambridge Univ. Press, 1987) Pages 49-66, 119-171

Gregory, Andrew *An Oral and Written Gospel? Reflections on Remembering Jesus:
The Expository Times vol. 116* (September, 2005) Pages 7-12

Halpern, Baruch *Eyewitness Testimony: Parts of Exodus Written Within Living Memory of the
Event Biblical Archaeology Review vol. 29* (2003) Pages 50-57

Heinemann, Joseph *Prayer in the Period of the Tanna'im and the Amora'im: Its Nature and its Patterns* (Jerusalem: Magnes Press, 1984) Pages 1-12

Hollander, Harm *The Words of Jesus: From Oral Traditions to Written Record: Novum Testamentum vol. 32* (MA: Brill Press, 2000) Pages 340-357

Ito, Akio *The Written Torah and the Oral Gospel: Novum Testamentum vol. 37* (MA: Brill Press, 2006) Pages 234-260

Jaffee, Martin S. *Early Judaism* (NJ: Prentice Hall Press, 1997) Pages 1-91

Jaffee, Martin S. *Torah in the Mouth: Writing and Oral Tradition in Palestinian Judaism 200 BCE-400 CE* (New York: Oxford University Press, 2001) Pages 3-5, 17-18, 68-72, 101-109, 124-126, 130-132

Jones, Cheslyn *The Study of Liturgy* (NY: Oxford University Press, 1997)

Kadushin, Max *Organic Thinking* (NY: The Jewish Theological Seminary of America, 1938)

Kaplan, Aryeh *Meditation and the Bible* (ME: Weiser Press, 1988) Pages 1-61

Kebler, Werner *The Words of Memory: Memory, Tradition, and Text* (GA: SBL Press, 2005) Pages 219-248

Kennedy, George *New Testament Interpretation through Rhetorical Criticism* (NC: North Carolina Press, 1984) Pages 12-13, 68-69

Klein, Michael L. *Targumic Texts as Mnemonic Device* (Jerusalem: HUC) Page 1

Koester, Helmut *Ancient Christian Gospels* (PA: Trinity Press, 1990) Pages 30-55

Koester, Helmut *Written Gospels or Oral Tradition? In Journal of Biblical Literature vol. 113* (GA: SBL Press, 1994) Pages 293-297

Krueger, Derek *Writing and the Liturgy of Memory: In Journal of Early Christian Studies vol. 8* (John Hopkins Press: 2000) Pages 483-510

Landman, Leo *The Cantor: An Historic Perspective* (NY: Yeshiva University Press, 1972) Pages 1-50

Leclercq, Jean *The Love of Learning and the Desire for God, a Study of Monastic Culture* (NY: Fordham Press, 1977) Pages 1-308

Lichthcim, Miriam *Ancient Egyptian Literature Vol. 2* (CA: Univ. of California Press, 1976) Pages 148, 149

Lieberman, Saul *Greek in Jewish Palestine* (PA: JPS Press, 1942) Pages 1-114

Lieberman, Saul *Hellenism in Jewish Palestine* (PA: Jacoby Press, 1950) Pages 83-97

Lord, Albert *The Gospels as Oral Traditional Literature: In the Relationships Among the Gospels* (TX: Trinity Univ. Press, 1973) Pages 33-91

Lord, Albert *The Singer of Tales* (MA: Harvard Press, 1964) Pages 26-29, 97-98

Mack, John *The Museum of the Mind* (UK: The British Museum Press, 2003) Pages 39-51

Maxwell, Jaclyn *Pedagogical Methods in John Chrysostom's Preaching Studia Patristica vol. XLI* (MA: Peeters Press, 2006) Pages 445-450

McVey, Kathleen *Ephrem the Syrian Hymns* (NY: Paulist Press, 1989) Pages 1-468

Morgan, Robert *James Dunn's Jesus Remembered The Expository Times vol. 116* (2005) Pages 1-6

Morris, Nathan *The Jewish School* (London: Eyre and Spottiswoode Press, 1937) Pages 112-165

Nielsen, Edward *Oral Tradition* (London: SCM Press, 1961) Pages 1-103

Neisser, Ulric *Memory Observed* (CA: W.H. Freeman, 1982) Pages 311-314

Neusner, Jacob *Oral Tradition in Judaism: The Case of the Mishnah* (NY: Garland Publishing, 1987) Pages 61-98

Neusner, Jacob *The Memorized Torah: the Mnemonic System of the Mishnah* (CA: Scholars Press, 1985)

Neusner, Jacob *The Rabbinic Traditions About the Pharisees Before A.D. 70: The Problem of Oral Transmission In: Journal of Jewish Studies vol. 22* (NY: Jcwish Chronicle Publications, 1971) Pages 1-18

Neusner, Jacob *Understanding Rabbinic Judaism* (NY: Ktav Publishing, 1974)

Niditch, Susan *Oral World and Written Word* (KY: Westminster John Knox Press, 1996)
Pages 1-134

Nielsen, Edward *Oral Tradition: A Modern Problem in Old Testament Introduction*
(London: SCM Press, 1954)

Patrich, Joseph *Sabas, Leader of Palestinian Monasticism* (Dumbarton Oaks: DC, 1995)
Pages 229-253

Porter, Stanley E. *Handbook of Classical Rhetoric in the Hellenistic Period*
(NY: Brill Press, 1997) Pages 159-167

Price, R.M. *Lives of the Monks of Palestine* (MI: Cistercian Publications, 1991) Pages 1-111

Osborn, E.F. *Teaching and Writing in the First Chapter of the Stromateis In:*
The Journal of Theological Studies vol. 9 (London: Oxford Press, 1958) Pages 335-343

Osiek, Carolyn *The Oral World of Early Christianity in Rome* (MI: Eerdmans Press, 1998)
Pages 151-172

Pedersen, Kirsten Stoffregen *Traditional Ethiopian Exegesis of the Book of Psalms*
(Germany: Wiesbaden, 1995)

Porter, Stanley *Reading the Gospels Today* (MI: Eerdmans Publishing, 2004) Pages 56-76

Riesner, Rainer *Jesus and the Oral Gospel Tradition* (England: Sheffield Press, 1991)
Pages 185-210

Ringgren, Helmer *Oral and Written Transmission in the O.T. In: Studia Theologica vol. 3*
(Germany: Lund Press, 1950) Pages 34-59

Roberts, C.H. *The Codex* (Londres: Oxford Press, 1983) Pages 169-204

Rops, Daniel *Daily Life in Palestine at the Time of Christ* (London: Morrison Press, 1962)
Pages 269-271

Roskies, David *A Bridge of Longing* (MA: Harvard University Press, 1995)

Ross-Larson, Bruce *Edit Yourself: A manual for Everyone Who Works with Words W.W.*
    (NY: Norton Press, 1982)

Safrai, Shmuel *The Literature of the Sages* (PA: Fortress Press, 1987)

Safrai, Shmuel *The Sayings of Hillel: Their Transmission and Reinterpretation In: Hillel and Jesus*
    (1997) Pages 321-334

Schaff, Philip *Nicene and Post-Nicene Fathers* (MI: Eerdmans Publishing, 1979)

Schaper, Joachim *Memory in the Bible and Antiquity: The Living Word Engraved in Stone*
    (Germany: Siebeck Press, 2007) Pages 9-21

Schniedewind, William *How the Bible became a Book* (NY: Cambridge Press, 2004) Pages 1-17

Schultz, Hans Jürgen *Jesus in His Time* (MN: Fortress Press, 1971)

Silver, Daniel Jeremy *The Story of Scripture* (NY: Basic Books, 1990)
        Pages 1-54, 209-214

Stewart, William *Oral Tradition: The Expository Times vol. 68* (1957) Page 284

Talstra, Eep *Unless Someone Guide Me: Texts for Recitation*
    (Netherlands: Shaker Publishing, 2001) Pages 67-76

Veilleux, Armand *Pachomian Koinonia vol. 1* (MI: Cistercian Press, 1980) Pages 30, 31, 38, 39,
        58, 59, 86, 87, 100, 101, 116, 117, 134-137, 144, 145, 158-161, 194, 195, 202-205,
        212-215, 230-237, 254, 255, 264, 265, 338-341, 356, 357, 452, 453

Veilleux, Armand *Pachomian Koinonia vol. 2* (MI: Cistercian Press, 1981)
        Pages 30, 31, 86-89, 128, 129, 142-157, 162-167, 190-195, 200-211

Veilleux, Armand *Pachomian Koinonia vol. 3* (MI: Cistercian Press, 1982) Pages 16, 17, 114-117

Walls, A.F. *Papias and Oral Tradition: Vigiliae Christianae vol. 21* (1967) Pages 136-140

Wansbrough, Henry *Jesus and the Oral Gospel Tradition* (UK: Sheffield Press, 1991)

Watson, Wilfred *Classical Hebrew Poetry a Guide to its Techniques* (England: Sheffield Academic Press, 1995)

Williams, Joseph M *Style: Ten Lessons in Clarity and Grace* (IL: Scott Foresman Press, 1989)

Wire, Antoinette Clark *Holy Lives, Holy Deaths, a Close Hearing of Early Jewish Storytellers: Society of Biblical Literature* (2002) Pages 1-23